CARDINAL IDEAS OF ISAIAH

BOOKS BY DR. JEFFERSON

QUIET TALKS WITH THE FAMILY
QUIET TALKS WITH EARNEST PEOPLE
QUIET HINTS TO GROWING PREACHERS
THE MINISTER AS PROPHET
THE MINISTER AS SHEPHERD
CHRISTIANITY AND INTERNATIONAL PEACE
DOCTRINE AND DEED
THINGS FUNDAMENTAL
THE CHARACTER OF JESUS
THE NEW CRUSADE
BUILDING OF THE CHURCH
WHY WE MAY BELIEVE IN LIFE AFTER DEATH
TALKS ON HIGH THEMES
THE CAUSE OF THE WAR
A FIRE IN THE SNOW
THE LAND OF ENOUGH
AN ORIGINAL YEAR
CONGREGATIONALISM
WHAT THE WAR IS TEACHING
SOLDIERS OF THE PRINCE
FORE-FATHERS' DAY SERMONS
UNDER TWENTY
THE FRIENDSHIP INDISPENSABLE
THE CHARACTER OF PAUL
FIVE PRESENT-DAY CONTROVERSIES
WHAT THE WAR HAS TAUGHT US
OLD TRUTHS AND NEW FACTS

CARDINAL IDEAS
OF ISAIAH

BY

CHARLES E. JEFFERSON

New York

THE MACMILLAN COMPANY

1925

PRINTED IN THE UNITED STATES OF AMERICA BY
THE CORNWALL PRESS

CONTENTS

CARDINAL IDEAS OF ISAIAH

THE CARDINAL IDEAS OF ISAIAH

I

THE VALUE OF THE STUDY OF THE HEBREW PROPHETS

There is an impression in the minds of many that modern scholarship has taken away our Bible, and one can readily understand why such an idea should get abroad. When the scholars told us that Moses did not write the Pentateuch, and that David wrote hardly any of the Psalms, perhaps none, and that Isaiah, the son of Amoz, did not write half of the book which bears his name, and that the Book of Job is a dramatic poem, and that the Song of Solomon is a love poem, and that the Book of Jonah is an allegory, and that the Book of Daniel is a specimen of apocalyptical literature, full of glowing symbolism but destitute of historic value, one is not surprised that many people concluded that the Bible had been taken away. When these scholars insisted on our reading certain sentences in the Pentateuch under the blazing light of scientific discovery, and when they went on to point out contradictions and discrepancies in the historical books which no in-

February 8, 1925.

genuity can possibly reconcile, it is no wonder that many persons felt that the very foundations of the Christian religion had been removed. But now that we have had time to recover somewhat from our panic, we have come to see that the Bible has not been taken away from us at all. If it was taken away from us by modern scholarship, it was only for a moment, and modern scholarship has handed it back to us again more useful and precious than ever. The whole Bible has been handed back, and a new light shines from its pages. The fact is that a considerable portion of the Bible had gotten away from us before modern scholarship had begun its work. We had lost the Prophets. We very seldom read them. We did not read them because we did not understand them.

I am speaking to a fairly representative congregation of Christian people. You have been brought up in various communions of the Great Church of Christ. You have been reared and educated in different sections of the country—some of you in New England, some in the South, some in the Middle West, and others in the Far West—and I have no doubt that if you were subjected to an examination on the Prophets, you would give substantially the same answers. If I should ask you, Have you been a diligent student of the Prophets? Have you taken great interest in the Prophets? Have you experienced delight in the reading of the Prophets? Have you made a specialty of the Prophets, so you can tell what distinctive contribution each one of them made to the religious thought of the world? I presume you would all give the same answer—"No!"

For a long time a quarter of the Old Testament—the prophetical portion—was little more than a Sahara Desert. To be sure there was an oasis here and there on which green things were growing, and where we could find food and refreshing. There were isolated paragraphs, scattered sentences which gave us strength and inspiration, but for the most part, the whole region extending from Isaiah to Malachi, was little more than sand. Modern scholarship has irrigated this desert and made it to blossom as the rose. I want to study a portion of it with you on the coming Sunday mornings. I invite you to study with me the prophecies of Isaiah, the son of Amoz.

I can imagine what reaction you give to such an announcement. Some of you are already saying, "What an uninteresting and unprofitable subject. Why should we give our attention to a man who lived and died so many centuries ago? In a world like ours, crowded with fascinating personalities, why should we give our thought to a Jew who has been in his grave 2600 years? In an age so bristling with interesting and baffling problems, why should we turn aside to think about this seer of ancient Israel?" It is a natural question for any man to ask. I do not wonder that you ask it, and here is my answer to it. Isaiah was a man of genius, one of the great religious geniuses of our race. Many regard him as the greatest of all the Hebrew Prophets. The only one who can possibly present a stronger claim to preëminence is the Prophet Jeremiah. This man Isaiah had amazing insight, and extraordinary courage. He was a man of genius, and therefore, it is well worth while to get near him. You cannot get close to a man of genius without being quickened and illumined by him. And as for him living so many centuries ago, that is a great help in our study of him. It is a mistake to suppose that you cannot understand a man who has been dead a long while. It is not until a great man has been dead a long while, that you really see him as he is. In the study of great men, it is as with the study of portraits painted in oil. You have no doubt had this experience. You have stood within a few inches of an oil portrait of some man, and you have not been able to see the man at all. All that you could see was some pigment smeared upon a piece of canvas. You could see paint and nothing more. But now stand back—stand back a little farther, and now still farther. You notice that at every step backward, the man comes out to meet you. He comes up out of the paint, and after you have gone back far enough, you can see his features. But now stand back, stand back still farther, and you get something more than his features, you get the spiritual expression of his soul. Just so it is in the study of great men—stand too close to them and you cannot see them. You must stand back a long distance in order to get the expression of their mind and heart. We cannot understand Theodore Roosevelt and Woodrow Wilson. They are as yet too close to us. We cannot measure accurately the stature of Lloyd George or Ramsay MacDonald. The world must wait until they have been dead a hundred years. We can see far more distinctly and appreciate far more truly Washington and Lincoln than any of these four men just now named. Washington has been in his grave one hundred and twenty-five years, and that is the reason we know him so well. Lincoln has been dead sixty years, and we are just beginning to enter into a proper appreciation of his mighty soul.

The fact that Isaiah has been dead 2600 years is no handicap in our study of the man. He was a great figure in the eighth century before Christ, and because he is so far removed from us, we can get very near to him. We are greatly helped by the fact that his body has vanished. The physical part of the man has entirely disappeared. We do not know anything of the color of his eyes or the shape of his nose or his chin. We know nothing of his beard or his moustache or his hair. We know nothing of his girth or his stature. The whole physical man is gone, and that helps us. These physical features are distracting. They keep our mind away from the man's message. Isaiah to us is nothing but a voice, and that helps us to concentrate our whole mind upon his ideas. Moreover his family and political connections have all vanished. We know nothing of his father or his mother, his brothers and sisters, his uncles and aunts, his wife and his children. This is an advantage. If we knew any of these, or all of them, they would obstruct our view. We should find ourselves thinking again and again of them. The people of Galilee were handicapped in their dealing with Jesus, because they knew his father and mother, his brothers and sisters. They would have been able to come closer to him if his whole family had been swept out of sight. Moreover, we are so far removed from Isaiah that his mannerisms do not repel us. Every man has mannerisms, and sometimes they are disagreeable. Isaiah, of course, had mannerisms. He employed methods which no doubt would have offended us. At one period in his life he walked for three years through the streets of Jerusalem clad in an old shirt, the sort of shirt which slaves wore, in order to symbolize to the eyes of his countrymen that they, unless they changed their course, would some day wear the shirts of slaves. If we had lived in Jerusalem and had seen that man wearing an old shirt, we should probably have done what many of the citizens of Jerusalem did, put him down as a fanatic or a lunatic, but we are so far removed from him that we are not offended by that shirt. It has been transmuted by a subtle magic into a silken garment of an ambassador of the King of Heaven. It is with that shirt as it is with the crown of thorns which Jesus wore on the day of his crucifixion. To the people of Jerusalem it was a crown of thorns and nothing more, but we, looking through the mists of 1900 years, see that it is a crown of glory. Distance greatly helps one in the study of a great man.

Possibly some one is saying, "Why should we study the problems of a little nation so insignificant as Judah?" The whole of Palestine was no larger than the State of Connecticut, and Judah covered only the southern third of the country. Jerusalem was little more than a shabby and primitive village—nothing at all compared with the great capitals of our day. The people were economically poor and numerically small and politically insignificant, and so it is only natural that the question should rise, "Why should we bother ourselves with the triumphs and defeats, the political combinations of a little nation that has long since passed away?" The answer to that question is that it is not necessary to have a great nation if your purpose is to study human nature. If you are interested in the operation of political ideas, and wish to analyze political combinations and movements, you do not need an empire of a hundred million people. Just a little nation of a few hundred thousand will do as well, if not better. When a chemist wants to learn something about water, he does not need the Atlantic Ocean. If he desires to get the constituent elements

of water, and to know how oxygen and hydrogen
behave, all he asks for is a cup of water. A physicist
in his study of water does not ask for an ocean in
order to find out what happens when water boils, and
what happens when water freezes. A pail of water
is enough. He can tell from a pail of water far
more successfully than he can from the ocean. Just
so in the study of social and political problems. We
do not need a great stage or millions of people. We
do better if the stage is contracted and the population is comparatively small.

There was another ancient people, very small and
politically insignificant—the Greek. It played its
part on a small stage, and yet who would say that it
is not worth our while to study it? That little nation has left its mark on humanity for all time. When
you go to the theater, all the words in use there are
from Greece. "Theater" is Greek, so is "Drama,"
so is "Tragedy," so is "Comedy." "Prologue" and
"Dialogue" and "Epilogue," all are Greek. The
"Orchestra" is Greek, and so is the "Chorus," and so
is the "Scenery," and so is the word "Characters."
The Greeks were a small nation acting their part on
a small stage, but they put a stamp upon the theater,
which will not be effaced during the next ten thousand years. They marked it once and forever. It
is a most amazing fact that this Grecian people,
numerically small, economically poor, and politically
insignificant, created and developed every form of
poetry and every form of prose. The Greeks laid

down the lines along which European literature has moved, and in the course of more than 2000 years, literature has not been able to add to the forms which that amazing people invented. Do not sniff then at a nation because it is small. Great men can play great parts on a small stage, and little nations can become the incarnation of the ideas of the Eternal. It is well worth our while to study ancient Greece, and it is equally worth our while to study ancient Judah.

There is a third question which may arise in certain minds. I can imagine I hear some one saying, "How is the study of Isaiah going to help me? Of what value will it be to me in my business or in my work?" We Americans are intensely practical people, and we do not want to study anything that we cannot turn to immediate use. I can understand how an American might feel that no advantage could come to him from a study of the Book of Isaiah. In answer to that question, let me say that while in superficial ways the world of Isaiah is not the world in which we live, nevertheless in other ways the world has not changed at all. The material civilization of the eighth century before Christ was in marked contrast with the material civilization which we know. When we look upon Isaiah's world, and then look upon our world, we say, "Heaven and earth have passed away, and all things have become new." And yet when we look more deeply, we can see that Isaiah's world still abides.

[9]

God has not changed. He is still King of Kings and Lord of Lords. The laws of God have not been altered. They are today what they have always been. The law of gravitation has not changed, nor has the law of righteousness. Cause and effect are still linked together, as they were when Isaiah lived. The penalties of sin and the rewards of righteousness, these go on from generation to generation without variation or shadow of turning. And while God remains the same, so also does human nature. Men have changed within 2600 years only in superficial ways. The human heart is now what it has always been. No new instinct has been added to our nature within the last 2600 years. No new appetite has been generated. No new passion has been introduced. The instincts and appetites and passions with which the modern psychologist is dealing, are the same instincts and appetites and passions with which Isaiah had to deal. We are living in a new world, but the new world is old. The sins which men commit today are the sins which men committed 2600 years ago. The social evils with which we grapple are the social evils with which Isaiah wrestled. If you make out a list of the sins of Isaiah's day, and then a list of the sins of our day, and put the lists side by side, you will see that they are identical; and therefore, it is foolish to suppose that we have nothing to learn from the study of human society as it existed 2600 years ago. It is impossible to study the life of the eighth century before Christ without getting instruction which will help us in living our life and doing our work.

And now let us turn to the question, Who is a Prophet—what is the meaning of that word "Prophet"? We all know its meaning in our current speech. We never use it except in one sense. We always means a predictor—a foreteller—a man who tells what is going to happen. We have men who predict the weather. They tell you today what the weather will be tomorrow. Sometimes they wax bold, and tell you what the weather will be a week in advance. Sometimes they become almost audacious and tell you what a season is going to be. It will be cold or hot. It will be dry or wet. But the weather prophets do not enjoy an enviable reputation. They often prophesy things that do not happen. We have another kind of prophet in our midst, the man who tells you when the end of the world is coming. Every generation has that sort of prophet. One would suppose that that particular kind of foolery would some day die out, but there is no evidence thus far that it ever will die out. In each succeeding generation men arise to announce the end of the world. Of course they do not know anything about it. No one can know anything about it. Any man who claims the ability to name the date of the end of the world is an impostor or fanatic. Some wag has given us this definition of a prophet: "He is a man who predicts things that never happen." The popular meaning of the word

"Prophet," therefore, is a foreteller of future events. But that is not the Biblical meaning of the word.

According to the Bible a prophet is one who speaks for another. This comes out in an alleged conversation between God and Moses. It is recorded in the Book of Exodus that God wants Moses to do a certain thing, and Moses is trying to back out. He says that he cannot speak. Whereupon God says to him, "Your brother Aaron will be your prophet; that is, he will be your spokesman. I will give you ideas, and your brother Aaron will give these ideas expression. He will speak for you. He will be your prophet." That is the Biblical significance of "Prophet" everywhere.

A religious prophet is a man who speaks for God. Isaiah is called a prophet because he spoke for God. To be sure he sometimes predicted. No religious teacher can keep his tongue off the future altogether. Man is a creature who lives in the past, the present, and the future, and it is impossible to deal with the past and present without dealing more or less with the future. All the Old Testament prophets now and then predicted, but that was not their main business. Their main business was not with the future, but with the present. They were interpreters of experience, the experience through which their countrymen were passing. To them events were words of the Lord, and they were called to explain the meaning of these events to the people. Experience is the medium of revelation. It is in the things that we suffer that God makes his will known. God does not speak clearly to the average man through human experience, and the work of the prophet is to tell men what this experience means. Jesus was a Prophet, the greatest of all. He always spoke for God. He explained to men what God was saying in nature and in history and in the human heart. He chided the religious teachers of his day because they had degenerated into weather prophets. They knew how to talk about the weather, but they were unable to discern the signs of the times. The great social movements of their day were unintelligible to them. Things were taking place of momentous significance, and the significance was all lost upon them. For instance, they kept talking about the return of Elijah, and yet John the Baptist stood before them, and they did not know that Elijah had come; that is, they could not recognize the reappearance of old forces, when the old forces showed themselves under new forms. Isaiah was a prophet, not an ordinary prophet, but an extraordinary one. The Hebrew race produced possibly thousands of prophets, but the names of only a few of them have been preserved. Isaiah was one of the greatest of them all. He read the life of the eighth century, giving it a spiritual interpretation, which is one of the inestimable treasures of our race. His interpretation is well worth our study.

The supreme value of the study of the Hebrew prophets is that it helps to make our Bible a living book. To many of us, possibly to most of us, the Bible is a dead book. That is the reason we read it so little. If it were a living book we would read it. Being a dead book we neglect it. The Bible is a voice, but to many it is a dead voice. It is a voice that comes up out of the tomb. If it were a living voice we would pay attention to it. It is lamentable how little influence the Bible exerts on the conduct of the average Christian. This is because the Bible is a dead book, and not a living book. When we read the "Arabian Nights," we find ourselves in a land of enchantment. Everything takes place by magic. Children like that sort of a book, and we older people also like it. It does us good now and then to get away from this old prosaic, mechanical world, and revel in the freedom of a world that is magical. There is no connection between the magical world and this world. Living in that magical world does not help us to run our homes or conduct our business or administer our church, but it is fun to get away from life's everlasting routine, and live for just an hour in a world in which all natural laws are suspended and everything takes place by magic. There are many people who read the Bible just as they read the "Arabian Nights." The Bible is a different world to the world in which they are living. The Bible is a supernatural world—a world in which miracles occur—a world in which God is talking and acting all the time. God says this and that and the other thing. God does this and that and something else. God blesses this one, punishes that one, exalts this one, pulls another down. The whole Bible world is full of God. It is very interesting to learn what God said and did. After we have spent an hour in this supernatural world, we close the Bible and come out into a world altogether different. It is a prosaic world where everything goes on according to natural law. God is not saying anything. God is not doing anything. All that is done and said is done and said by men. There is just as great a distance between the Bible world and the world in which we live, as between our world and the world of Aladdin. The "Arabian Nights" do not help us to live in New York City, nor does the Bible either. Many business men read the Bible, but the Bible does not influence their business policy. Many politicians read the Scriptures, but the Scriptures do not modify or control their platform or their program. The Bible is a sort of "Arabian Nights." Men lose themselves for a time in it and find it interesting as a fairy story, and then come back into this prosaic everyday world, to live and act as though they had never seen the Bible.

How can we make the Bible a living book? That is one of the great tasks of a preacher. There is no finer thing that a preacher can do, nor is there a more difficult thing for him to do, than to convert the Bible into a living book, so to deal with it as to make it speak with a living voice. The Bible world and our world are not really different at all. God does not change. He is speaking all the time. He is speaking as distinctly and clearly now as he has ever spoken. He as acting now. He is acting as constantly and effectively today as he has ever acted. We are living in a supernatural world, and miracles are happening all the time. It would be absurd to suppose that God spoke in the eighth century and is dumb in the twentieth century. If he ever spoke at all, he is surely speaking today. Tell me that he is not speaking today and then I will refuse to believe that he ever spoke. It would be incredible to suppose that he spoke to men in Jerusalem, and that he will not speak to men in New York City. God is speaking and acting every day and every night. He is saying things to us hour by hour. Everything depends upon our eyes and our ears. Our Lord was in the habit of saying, "He that hath ears to hear, let him hear." People were deaf in his day. They could not hear what God was saying. People are deaf in our day. They do not catch the accents of the divine voice. In the last book of the New Testament, there is a sentence which occurs again and again like a recurring and haunting refrain, "He that hath ears to hear, let him hear what the Spirit is saying—what the Spirit is saying— what the Spirit is saying. He that hath ears to hear, let him hear!"

II

WHY IT IS DIFFICULT TO READ THE PROPHETS

There is no doubt the Prophets are difficult to read. You know from your own experience that they constitute the most difficult portion of the Old Testament Scriptures. They are the most valuable section of the Old Testament and have the most to give us, but nevertheless they give us the least. We get little from them, because they are so hard to read, and by reading I mean reading in the deepest sense. We sometimes use the word "read" in a superficial way. We mean pronouncing the words, or running the eyes over the printed sentences. A man says that he reads a chapter of the Bible every night. That may mean much, or it may mean little. He may mean that he runs his eyes over the sentences in a chapter, or he may mean that he runs the sentences through his mind in such a way as to cause the sentences to drop their meaning into his mind. You have heard people say that they have read the Bible through twenty times. That may mean much or little. It depends entirely upon how they read. One can run his eyes up and down the

February 15, 1925.

pages of the Bible and be little the better for it. It is singular how superstition keeps creeping into our lives. By superstition I mean irrational ideas and practices. In the middle ages many pious people went on pilgrimages to the shrine of some famous saint. They would walk miles and miles in order to gaze on a finger bone or an ankle bone of some holy man of old. They would travel far to kiss some object that a saint had touched. After the Reformation that form of foolishness subsided somewhat, and men began to act in another superstitious way. They began to read the Bible through. They made a yearly pilgrimage from Genesis to the Apocalypse. It was not so futile a superstition as the one which carried men on pilgrimages to holy shrines, but in many cases it was a waste of time. You have probably heard your grandmother say that she had read the Bible through thirty times, but alas, much that she read meant nothing to her. It is not the reading of the Bible that matters, but the understanding of it. It is not worth while to read unless we understand. We must work common sense into our religion. Paul was a man of common sense. There were people in the City of Corinth who nettled him not a little. They were very pious and persisted in saying things which nobody understood. He told them that he wanted to pray with his mind—that he wanted to sing praise with his mind, and that when he spoke he wanted to speak with his mind so that other people could understand what he was saying. "I would rather speak five words with my mind," he declared in his strong way, "than ten thousand words in a tongue which nobody can comprehend." It is better to read five sentences in the Bible with your mind, than ten thousand sentences with your eyes. There are many people who imagine they are better off if they have a Bible in the house. They would be ashamed not to have a Bible in the house. Because they have a Bible in the house, they think that God must be well pleased with them. The important thing is not to have a Bible in the house, but to have the Bible in the mind. If the Bible is not in the mind, it does not make any difference whether it is in the house or not. A Bible in the house may be worth nothing more than an old horse shoe. You all, I presume, have the prophets in your house, but the question is, have you the prophets in your mind? It is difficult to get them into one's mind. Let us ask ourselves this morning, the reason why.

You yourself have sometimes offered an explanation. You have been quite self-deprecatory, and have said that you could not understand the prophets because of your stupidity. You have taken all the blame upon yourself. You are convinced that you have not brains enough to understand such deep reading. You have attributed the whole difficulty to your own intellectual dullness. But I do not think that that is a correct explanation. Others of you have felt that you cannot understand the Prophets, because you are not good enough. You have read in one of Paul's letters, that the natural man cannot understand spiritual things because they are spiritually discerned, and you know that you are not very spiritual. You have read in another Letter, that "To be carnally minded in death," and you feel that you are so carnally minded that it is death to your understanding of the Prophets. I do not think that that is a sound explanation. I feel sure the difficulty lies in another quarter. I want to point out six reasons why the Prophets are difficult to understand.

The first reason is that we have an imperfect Hebrew text. The tooth of time is ceaselessly at work, and it has eaten through many of the ancient manuscripts, so that here and there a word is partially obliterated, and in other cases it is completely gone. Dr. Moffatt, who has just gotten out a new translation of the Old Testament, says in his preface that, "The Masoretic or traditional text of the Old Testament is often desperately corrupt." He means by that, that it is regrettably ragged. Time has chewed the manuscript in such a way as to make it well-nigh impossible here and there to find the meaning of the author, and so Dr. Moffatt candidly confesses that in many places he has been obliged to guess. When guessing has been possible, he has guessed, but when guessing has not been possible, he has put a line of dots to indicate that it is impossible for him even to conjecture what the original sentence meant. There are sentences scattered here and there through the Prophets which make no sense at all.

A second reason is faulty translation. The King James Version was made in the 17th century, and in many ways it is a most excellent version, but at various points it is quite defective, and therefore when you read the Prophets you should always read the translation of the Revisers. Textual criticism has made great advances within the last three hundred years, and things which were obscure in the reign of King James I have been cleared up by the indefatigable industry of Bible scholars. But even the revised version is by no means perfect. It is always difficult to decide what English word is the exact equivalent of a Hebrew word, and the judgments of scholars on such matters frequently differ. Because of this difficulty, no translation of the Bible is ever altogether satisfactory. Sentences occur in which you cannot be sure that you have gotten hold of the English words which express the author's meaning. Some of the difficulty in reading the Prophets arises from the fact that the translator blundered.

A more baffling form of difficulty is our inability sometimes to disentangle the words of the Prophet from the words of other people. Our translators have not taken the trouble to help us at that point. They do not use quotation marks as often as they should. Let me give you an illustration. In the 28th chapter of Isaiah, the Prophet is arraigning his countrymen for their drunkenness. His condemnation is hot. He says that even the Prophets and Priests are addicted to wine, and they drink so much that their eyes have become bleared, and their minds have become befuddled; and then he makes use of a very vigorous sentence, the kind of sentence which he does not hesitate to use when he wants to express his feeling. He says that these men vomit over everything, so that there is no place that is clean. He says that in the 8th verse. In the 9th verse he goes on to say, "Whom will he teach knowledge? And whom will he make to understand the message —them that are weaned from the milk, and drawn from the breasts?" In the 10th verse, he says, "For it is precept upon precept, precept upon precept; line upon line, line upon line; here a little, there a little." The 11th verse reads, "Nay, but by men of strange lips and with another tongue will he speak to this people." Now what does that all mean? It means absolutely nothing to the average reader. The average reader makes nothing at all out of those four sentences. The reason why he does not understand them is because he does not see that the Prophet is speaking in verse 8, that the drunkards are speaking in verses 9 and 10, and that the prophet is speaking again in verse 11. If you will only make that distinction, the meaning comes out at once. The Prophet is condemning these drunkards. He is lashing them without mercy, and they get back at him. They mimic him. They are half tipsy, and in scornful tones they say, "Whom is this fellow trying to teach? Whom is he going to instruct by what he calls his message? Does he take us for babies? Does he treat us like so many children? He talks to us as though we were children in a kindergarten. It is always the same old story, precept upon precept, precept upon precept, line upon line, line upon line, here a little and there a little." And then the Prophet breaks in upon them and says, "Very well, by men of strange lips and another tongue" (that is by foreign soldiers who will speak a language which you do not understand), God will speak to you, and the monotony of his speech will be worse than the monotony of mine." The mimicry comes out far more vividly in the Hebrew because in the Hebrew you have nothing but monosyllables. The effect in English is somewhat spoiled by the recurring of the word "Precept," which is altogether too long. In the Hebrew these half tipsy men say, "Tsav-la-tsav, tsav-la-tsav, quav-la-quav, quav-la-quav, zeir-sham, zeir-sham." You must picture them wagging their head. You must catch the scorn of their mimicking voices, in order to get the force of these sentences. The Prophet breaks in on them by saying that God is going to talk some commonplaces, and that he will keep talking to them until they are broken to pieces and carried away captive.

Now we come to the chief reason why the Prophets are difficult to read. We must remember that the Prophets were preachers, and that there are two kinds of preaching. There is what we may call "Academic" preaching, the unfolding of ideas and truths for the sake of the ideas and truths themselves. A man may take a principle and unfold it, and explain it, illustrate it and adorn it, for the sheer joy of doing this. It is always an interesting work to take any idea or principle and give an exposition of it, unfolding its beauty, exploring its meaning. Many men rejoice in that sort of intellectual work, and many other people greatly enjoy seeing them do it. A preacher who preaches in this way does not apply his principle or his truth to the problems of society. He is not especially interested in conduct. He deals with his principle or truth in a vacuum and cares nothing about its relationships to the outside world. That is academic preaching. On the other hand, there is "Practical" preaching. When a man preaches practically, he always applies his ideas to the social or the political problems of his day. He is interested supremely in life, and the object of his preaching is to bring his ideas to bear upon life. This type of preacher is always grappling with the problems of his own generation, and is judging the movements of men by the principles which he proclaims. The Prophets were practical preachers. They never preached academically. They always applied their ideas to the life of their city and nation. They were easily understood by the people who heard them. Because they were easily understood by them, it is hard for us to understand them.

In order to know what they meant, we must be acquainted with the social and political conditions which they faced. We must get our eye on the target to know what they are driving at. We must understand the character of their opponents in order to appreciate the cleverness of their thrusts. We must be familiar with their historic environment in order to get the drift of their argument and feel the full force of their eloquence. The reason we find it so difficult to understand their language is because we are not acquainted with the world in which they lived. What you need, therefore, in reading the Prophets, is not more intellectual brilliancy, but more information. What you lack is not piety but light. I am, as you know, a practical preacher. I never preach academically. I am not interested in abstractions in the pulpit. In my library at home with books of philosophy around me, I can have a good time in the realm of theory and speculation, but as soon as I get into the pulpit, I am always practical; that is, I am always dealing with life as I see it around me. I care nothing for the unfolding of ideas unless I can apply them to the conduct of individuals and institutions. I am always preaching to the twentieth century. No other century has any controlling interest for me. I am preaching all the time to New York City. I am not especially interested in Philadelphia, Chicago, or San Francisco. I am always grappling with the intellectual and social and political problems which our generation is facing. And because I am a practical preacher my sermons would be difficult to read 2600 years from now. The Hebrew Prophets are difficult to read, because their preaching was so full of local color. The local color has been washed out by the rains of 2600 years. It has been bleached out by the suns of 2600 summers. My sermons are full of local color, and that local color will fade, so that my sermons will some day be hard to understand. Here and now they are easily understood. But just because my sermons are easily understood now, it would be difficult to understand them 2600 years from now. They are so full of references direct and remote; they are so crowded with allusions, sometimes subtle and sometimes obvious, that in order to read my sermons 2600 years from now, it would be necessary to make use of a dictionary, an encyclopedia, and a commentary. I am always referring to "Republicans," "Democrats," "Syndicalists," "Communists," "Anarchists," "Bolshevists." Again and again I say something about the "World Court," and the "League of Nations." Again and again I have spoken of the "Senate," and the "Subway Muddle," and the "18th Amendment." Some of the words I am using will become obsolete within the next 2600 years. Other words I am using will change their meaning within that period. In one of my sermons, I remember I said that the very year in which I came to New York the City enlarged the Tombs. What would people do with a sentence like that 2600 years from

now? They would have to look it up in an
encyclopedia. Occasionally I have referred to
"Hoboken." What a puzzle that would be! People
would not know whether that was the name of a
god or the name of a breakfast food. Open the Book
of Isaiah to chapter twenty-nine: "Ho Ariel!" Why
Ariel? You must look it up. You must recreate
Isaiah's world in order to understand Isaiah's words.
That, in a nutshell, is one reason why it is difficult
to read the Prophets.

There is another reason why it is difficult to read
them, and that is because the time sense of the ancient Hebrews was imperfectly developed. The time
sense is very strong in us. The clock plays a large
part in all our life. We carry a clock around with
us. Some of us even put it on our wrist, so that we
can see it often. We are very particular about dates
and seasons. The ancient Hebrew was an entirely
different kind of man. His mind did not work as
ours works. The man who wrote the first page of
Genesis said that God made Heaven and earth in
six days. He said something which to us is quite
shocking. We make a great ado about that. We
think he was fearfully ignorant, and committed an
egregious blunder. We are almost ready to give up
the whole Bible because he said such an absurd thing
as that. The fact is, it did not make the slightest
difference to him whether the world was made in
six days or six million years. That is not the point
which interested him. The only thing he cared any-

thing for was the fact that God created everything that was made. He lost himself in that great thought, and the time element was altogether incidental. We make a vast distinction between six days and six million years, and he cared nothing at all about it.

We are very particular about dates. We always date our letters. If we get a letter undated, we feel that the person who wrote to us left something undone. The Hebrews did not date their letters. Paul was a great letter writer, but never dated a letter, nor did Peter, nor did John, nor did any of the New Testament writers. It did not make any difference to them when they wrote them, nor did it make any difference to the people who got their letters. They were indifferent to the dates of events. We are punctilious on that point. We send our children to school to learn dates. We feel quite chagrined if now and then we forget a date. The Hebrews looked at events in a different way. For instance, they did not date the birth of Jesus, nor did they date his death. That to me is one of the most amazing facts in the whole world, that the Son of God should come into this world and live here, and work here, and die here, and that nobody should take the trouble to report either the year of his birth, or the year of his death. There is not a man upon this planet who knows today the year in which Jesus was born, or the year in which he died.

The Jews cared little for chronological sequence.

We are particular about matters of that sort. The temporal order is always of great importance to us. We want to begin at the beginning, and end at the ending, and put the intermediate matters between, but the Hebrew mind cared for none of those things.

You open the Book of Isaiah and think that you are beginning at the beginning, but you are not. We do not know just where we are in that chapter. The scholars are not agreed. Some think we are about in the middle of Isaiah's life, and some think we are well-nigh near the end. At any rate the first chapter is not the beginning. When we come to the 6th chapter, we find ourselves at the beginning. If we had been writing the Book of Isaiah, we would have put chapter six at the beginning. The Hebrews had a different kind of mind, and because their mind was different, we are always more or less confused and upset by their lack of attention to chronological sequence. They seem funny to us. Everybody seems funny who differs from us. They began reading a book at the end. They began reading a page from right to left. To us that seems ridiculous. When it came to dealing with numerals they were careless. You never can depend upon the chronology of the Books of the Old Testament. There are twenty-five numeral contradictions in one Old Testament Book, the Book of Numbers. The chronology of the Book of Isaiah is in a tangle. We know that he began to preach in the year in which Uzziah died, but we do not know in what year Uzziah died. We know approximately but not accurately. The Assyrians had the time sense highly developed. They were particular about their dates, and so we have been obliged to go to the cuneiform inscriptions on the Assyrian monuments to get light upon the chronological problems of the Old Testament. If Somebody should say, "Now why couldn't the Hebrews have been sensible? Why couldn't they have dated all important events, and arranged the chapters of their books in chronological sequence?" The Hebrews would have replied to a question like that, "Why cannot you be sensible—why do you make such an ado about the clock? Why are you always keeping your eyes on the clock? Why give to time an importance which it does not have? Why not think of ideas—of ideals which exist above the clock? Why should you be the slave of the calendar? Why not live in the realm of Eternal Truth?" If the Hebrews seem strange to us, we would seem still stranger to them. It may be they are right and that we are wrong. At any rate, you cannot depend upon the chronology of the Old Testament, and the prophets are all the more difficult for us to read because we grope our way without the assistance of fixed dates.

There is still another source of difficulty, and that is the lack of connection between the chapters, and sometimes the lack of connection between even the paragraphs of the same chapter. For instance, there is a gap between chapters 12 and 13, and another gap between chapters 23 and 24, and another gap between chapters 33 and 34. There is an enormous gap between chapters 39 and 40. That last gap is one of 150 years. The man who wrote the 40th chapter of Isaiah, lived at least 150 years after Isaiah, the Son of Amoz, was in his grave. Now how could a book ever be written in that way? What sort of a hodgepodge have we to deal with, when you cannot tell in one chapter what to expect in the next? We want continuity, running not only through the paragraphs of the chapter, but through all the chapters of a book. We will not tolerate gaps. We will not permit another author, unannounced, to push his ideas upon our attention right in the middle of a book written by somebody else.

In order to understand this singular phenomenon, we must bear in mind that the prophets were speakers and not writers. The earliest prophets wrote nothing at all. So far as we know, neither Elijah nor Elisha wrote a line. It is not until we come into the 8th century that we arrive at the so-called literary prophets. Whether Isaiah wrote much or not, we do not know. We know that Jeremiah wrote, and so also did Ezekiel, but beyond these we are not at all certain. We must never forget, either, that the oracles of the prophets were brief. An oracle was a message from God, and was nearly always short. The prophets were not philosophers. Philosophers deal in speculations and arguments, and these are sometimes elaborate and extended. The prophets were not scientists. Scientists deal in descriptions of observed phenomena, and these descriptions are often not brief. But the prophets were seers. They saw things. They sometimes saw a thing in a flash. In the twinkling of an eye, a great idea came upon them. In a moment they grasped a principle which they knew to be a principle of the Government of God. In a luminous hour they caught the vision of a sublime truth. A thought, an idea, a vision, can often be expressed in a few words, and therefore the oracles of the prophets are for the most part short.

In the third place, we must remember that the oracles were written down on strips of skin. They did not have paper as we have it, nor did they bind their writings into books like ours. Everything was written on strips of skin, and these strips of skin were rolled up. A book in those days was a roll of skin. Now these skins were expensive, and it was necessary to economize space, so that sometimes when a copyist had written down one or more oracles, there was a space of three or four inches still remaining. He could not allow that space to go to waste, and so he would write down another oracle. He would find one to fit that space. It did not matter to him whether it had any connection with the preceding oracles or not, nor did it always matter whether it was an oracle from the same prophet or not. If the divine messages were there, what difference did it make whether they were connected, or whether they were from the same man? They dealt with the oracles of the prophets very much as we deal with hymns. In our hymn book, hymn number 3 was written by Isaac Watts in the year 1719, and that hymn is followed by hymn number 4 which was written by Reginald Heber in the year 1827, one hundred and eight years later. We do not wonder at that. We put these two hymns together in our hymn book, and would not hesitate to use both of them in the same religious service. They are both upgushings of the heart—movements of gratitude and praise to the Almighty, and what objection is there to have them stand side by side in our hymn book? That is the way the copyists of Israel felt in regard to the oracles of the prophets. It was not necessary to have any connection between one and another. It was enough to believe that the oracles came through true prophets of God. After the copyists had done their work, these strips of skin were preserved by the scholars and leaders of the Hebrew Church, and it is not surprising that the skins would get mixed up, and that occasionally a prophet's name would disappear, so that an oracle would become anonymous. Men would forget the name of the prophet through whom that oracle came.

Somewhere about 200 B.C., the leaders of the Hebrew Church decided that they would collect all the prophetical writings of Israel into four books, and they decided to make these four books similar in size. The first book should bear the name "Isaiah," the second the name of "Jeremiah," the third the name of "Ezekiel," and the fourth should be called "The Book of the Twelve," including the prophets which we call the minor prophets. If you will take down your Bible some Sunday afternoon and examine these four books, you will see they are about the same size. Now, in order to make the Book of Isaiah equal in size to the Book of Jeremiah, it was necessary to bind up with the oracles of Isaiah, the son of Amoz, a number of other oracles written by different men. Just what was the principle of selection, we do not know, but probably these oracles were put all together because of the similarity in style. Isaiah, the son of Amoz was an orator. He was a master of language. His rhetoric is magnificent. His imagery is sometimes gorgeous. It was natural that the editors of Isaiah should include with his writings, other writings distinguished for their style. The Book of Isaiah is the most eloquent book in the Old Testament. Even if a man were not interested in the ideas of Isaiah, I should think he would be interested in it because of its language. Any man who is sensitive to the value of words, and who is moved by the splendors of speech, and who is entranced by that subtle melody of syllables which only the great orators know how to create, must be interested in the Book of Isaiah. And then, no doubt, similarity of attitude to life, and similarity of conception of God and men, must also have had something to do with bringing together the oracles which now constitute our Book of Isaiah.

In conclusion let me deal with a question which, no doubt, has arisen in the mind of more than one of you. What effect has all this on our idea of inspiration? We used to believe that the Bible was inspired. But what becomes of the doctrine of inspiration if the Bible is made up in such an apparently haphazard way? We used to think that the Bible was an authoritative book—a book of authority to our conscience, but what becomes of the doctrine of authority, when you have a book that is written by men all of whose names have been lost but one? That is a searching question deserving of serious consideration. When the composite authorship of Isaiah came to the attention of the scholars of fifty years ago, the first reaction was demoralization. Men were simply shocked. Theologians were stunned. It seemed as though the foundations were shaken. Many wondered if the doctrine of inspiration could be longer maintained. That, I think, is the first effect upon any mind. Any mind which becomes acquainted with the way in which the Bible took shape is very likely to be for a season upset and to feel that there is nothing solid upon which one can build. It takes time to adjust oneself to new facts. Some of us are stiff in our intellectual movements, and we do not adjust ourselves readily to anything that is new. But nevertheless we must accept facts however unpleasant, and we must adjust ourselves to them as readily as we can. There is nothing else to do. If we find it difficult to adjust ourselves to them, that is our infirmity, and not a virtue. A sensible man always adjusts himself to the facts. If the new facts render former doctrines incredible, then the former doctrines must go. Every lover of truth must stick close to the facts. If there are any whose confidence in the Bible is somewhat shaken by the facts brought to your attention this morning, let me make these two suggestions, first, the inspiration of a book is not invalidated by the discovery that it is anonymous. Anonymousness does not weaken the authority of a book. If anonymousness dissipates the idea of inspiration and robs the book of authority, then our Bible is hopelessly discredited. Who wrote the Book of Genesis? Nobody knows. To be sure, it is called "The First Book of Moses," but that title was not given it by its author. That was given it by an unknown editor, but it is no part of the book. The Book of Genesis is anonymous, and so is the Book of Exodus, and so is the Book of Leviticus, and so is the Book of Numbers, and so is the Book of Judges, and so is the Book of Ruth, and so is the Book of First Samuel, and so is the Book of Second Samuel, and so is the Book of First Kings, and so is the Book of Second Kings, and so is the Book of First Chronicles, and so is the Book of Second Chronicles, and so is the Book of Job, the greatest poem, according to Thomas Carlyle, that was ever written. So is the Book of Jonah, and so are other parts of the Old Testament. If anonymousness condemns a book, then the Bible is hopelessly condemned.

When you come to the New Testament, you will find a letter which is anonymous, the Letter to the Hebrews. Origen, the greatest scholar of the third century, who had access to all the sources of information in existence at that day, confessed, after long continued investigation, that he did not know who wrote that letter. "God only knows who wrote it," was his final comment. Modern scholars are obliged to say precisely what Origen said nearly 1700 years ago. It is the most eloquent letter in the New Testament. What are we going to do with it? Cast it out? No, we are going to keep it. Through that Letter God will always speak to the minds and hearts of men. Anonymousness does not discredit a book, or make it unworthy of a place in the Bible.

In the second place, let me suggest that every book must be judged by its content rather than by its alleged author. Do you want to know whether a book is inspired or not? You cannot tell simply by looking at the name of the man who is alleged to have written it. You can answer that question only by studying the content of the book. There are people who are very fond of a piece of music after they know who composed it. If it was composed by one of the great masters, then they take delight in it, but such people have no musical intelligence. Their opinion is worth nothing. There are people who love to hear a singer after they are informed that he gets five thousand dollars a night. They would not care to hear him if he did not get the five thousand dollars, but such people have no musical judgment. Anything they say about singing does not count. There are some people who do not care to look at a picture until somebody tells them it was sold for a hundred thousand dollars, and then they will stand before it for a long time declaring that it is wonderful—a masterpiece, but such people have no artistic insight. Their judgment counts for nothing. You must judge a piece of music by what it is. You must judge a singer by his voice and not by the box receipts. You must judge a painting by what it is, and not by the name that appears in the corner. Just so the books of the Bible must be judged not by the men who were alleged to have written them, but by the contents of the books themselves. A large part of the Book of Isaiah was written by men whose names have been lost, but the best minds of the Christian Church down through 1900 years have entertained the conviction that through the Book of Isaiah, God has spoken to the heart of mankind.

III

THE SOCIAL VISION OF ISAIAH

"The vision of Isaiah, the son of Amoz, which he saw concerning Judah and Jerusalem"; in other words, which he saw concerning his nation and his city. He saw things concerning them because he thought much about them. He carried them in his mind. It is the things which we carry in our mind which gather around them all sorts of ideas and wishes and dreams. He saw things concerning his country and his city because he bore them on his heart. He loved them, believed in them, and it was his love for them that gave new lenses to his eyes. It is love which enables us to see. A mother carries her boy upon her heart, and that is why she sees so many things concerning him—his welfare, his education, his future.

Isaiah has been thinking recently about Judah and Jerusalem more than usual. The King, the Great King Uzziah, is dead. Death is always solemnizing, more solemnizing perhaps to a man in the early twenties than it is in any other period of his life. As we grow older, we grow more accustomed to death. Almost every day we hear of the

February 22, 1925.

death of someone whom we have known. By and by we talk in this tone, "Your father lost a father. That father lost his, and therefore you must not grieve too much." King Uzziah was the greatest Hebrew King since Solomon. He had been on the throne for more than fifty years. We Americans do not know what that means. We have had twelve presidents within the last fifty years, and we kept no one of them long enough to become attached to him in the way in which the citizens of monarchies become attached to a good king who has reigned through two generations. Those of you who visited England within the last ten years of Queen Victoria's reign found something there, the like of which we have never had in this country, and never can have. There was a reverence for her, a devotion to her, and an affectionate worship of her which cannot be created in a Republic which changes its ruler every four years. Isaiah, like many another Jew, was devoted to King Uzziah, and now that Uzziah is dead, it seems as though the very Heavens have fallen. The young man does not know what is going to become of his country. A wind is blowing and there is no telling what it may blow to tatters. He hears the rumblings of subterranean fires and he cannot tell at what moment there may be an eruption of hot lava which will scorch Jerusalem to cinders. It is growing dark in Jerusalem, and in the darkness Isaiah sees things which he had never seen in the light. It is a singular thing that we can see some things better when it is dark, than when the sun is shining. For some things light is indispensable; for instance, the threading of a needle, or the finding of a coin which has rolled out of sight. The woman in the parable, as soon as she lost a piece of silver, lighted a candle and got her broom and began to sweep diligently in search of the treasure that was lost, and when at last the light fell upon the piece of silver coin, the coin laughed aloud, saying, "Here I am!" It was the light which brought the woman and the coin together. The astronomer works upon a different principle. He loves the dark, and when now and then the sun becomes dark in daytime, the astronomer rushes for his broom and sweeps diligently in search of the secrets that have escaped him in the light. We all know from our own experience, that we can see things in the dark.

"Who never ate his bread in sorrow,
Who never spent the darksome hours
Weeping and watching for the morrow
He knows you not, ye unseen Powers."

In the darkness Isaiah saw something he had never seen so clearly before—he saw God, and he saw his country and his city in the light which fell on them from God's face.

This heading of the first chapter of the Book of Isaiah, strikes the keynote of the whole book. If you will turn to the second chapter of the book, you will find the heading substantially the same as that of the first chapter—"the word that Isaiah, the son of Amoz, saw concerning Judah and Jerusalem." After the second chapter, this heading disappears, but the content of all the chapters from the beginning until chapter 13 is concerning Judah and Jerusalem. Those are Isaiah's two great themes. He never can get away from them. He thinks habitually of religion in civic and national terms. When you come to the 13th chapter, you observe that his vision widens, he now begins to see things concerning nations round about him. He has revelations concerning Babylon and Egypt and Ethiopia and Arabia and Moab and Damascus and Tyre. He sees things concerning all the nations around Judah, and all the foreign capitals within sight of Jerusalem. This man is an internationalist. He believes God is a God of cities as well as a God of individuals. He believes that God plans cities, builds cities, watches cities, sympathizes with cities, makes use of them in carrying out his eternal plans. Isaiah believes that God is interested in nations, that he plans them, waters them, trains them, desiring that they may bring forth blossoms which shall exhale the fragrance of Heaven. It is his purpose that nations shall produce fruit which shall feed and refresh the human heart. "Every man's life is a plan of God," so said Horace Bushnell over fifty years ago. Every city's life is a plan of God, and every nation's life is a plan of God, so thought Isaiah

2,600 years ago. My subject is "The Social Vision of Isaiah."

This is a profitable subject for study, because we have been brought up in a different school of religious thinking. We are individualists, more thoroughly individualistic in all our thinking than we realize. We talk, when we talk religiously, about men's souls. It is not easy for the most of us to talk about either cities or nations in the church. When we talk of those, we feel that we are getting out of the religious realm into the political. If one wants to know how individualistic we are in our thinking and feeling, all one has to do is to compare our hymn book with the hymn book of the Jewish Church. It is in the hymn book of a church that you find the heart of the church. The things which we sing about are the things which we carry in our hearts. And what is it that the Hebrews are always singing about? Open the Psalm Book almost anywhere and you will hear the choir singing about Jerusalem. Here is an illustration from the 48th Psalm: "Beautiful for situation, the joy of the whole earth is Mount Zion, on the sides of the north, the city of the great King. Walk about Zion and go round about her; Number the towers thereof; Mark ye well her bulwarks; consider her palaces; that ye may tell it to the generation following." In other words, count the towers and see how many there are. Take notice of the bulwarks and see how strong Jerusalem is. Let your mind dwell upon her palaces, that you may take in her magnificence and tell the story to your children. Do not allow this beautiful memory to die out, but hand it on as a glorious tradition from one generation to another." In that Psalm you get an expression of what was deep in the Hebrew heart. Or, take this from the 122d Psalm: "Pray for the peace of Jerusalem. They shall prosper that love thee. Peace be within thy walls, and prosperity within thy palaces. For my brethren and companions' sakes, I will now say, Peace be within thee." Or, take this from the 137th Psalm: "If I forget thee, O Jerusalem, let my right hand forget her cunning. If I do not remember thee, let my tongue cleave to the roof of my mouth." That is the way the Hebrew sang both in the temple and in the synagogue. That is not the way we Americans sing. We do not sing about our cities. We never sing of Washington City, beautiful though it is. We never sing about New York City. It is beautiful for situation, the greatest city in the New World, but we never sing about it. We never sing about the city in which we live, no matter what our city is. In our hymn book there is no hymn about a city. We scold about our cities— growl about them. We cudgel them—last them— sometimes stamp upon them in anger or in scorn. Possibly that is the reason why they are no better than they are. If we should stop kicking and cuffing them, and begin to sing about them, perhaps they might grow in grace and in the knowledge of Jesus Christ, our Savior. We accept Cowper's line as truth: "God made the country, Man made the town." And some of us believe that after God made the town, he turned it over to the devil, who has owned it ever since, and so we never bring our towns and cities within the circle of public worship. We leave them out in the outer darkness. We do not sing about them, because we do not have the social vision.

There are no hymns about cities in our hymn books, and only a few hymns about our nation. When you open the Jewish Psalm Book, you hear the choir always singing about the nation. The Jews had two names for their nation—one was "Jacob," and the other was "Israel." Glance up and down the pages of the Psalter, and see how many dozens of times those two words occur. There was nothing in which a Jew so exulted as in the opportunity to sing about his nation. Take the 105th and 106th Psalms—both of them great national hymns, both of them between fourteen and sixteen stanzas long when measured in the terms of our hymns. Our national hymns are short and very few in number. It is amazing how few we have. Our best loved national hymn is "My Country 'Tis of Thee." But we waited fifty-six years before we had that hymn, and then we had to wait seventy-two years more before Katherine Lee Bates wrote "America the Beautiful." We have three or four other hymns that are sung now and then, but one of them which

we often call a national hymn is not national at all—
Leonard Bacon's hymn, "O God, beneath Thy guid-
ing hand." That is a hymn for the Puritans of New
England. The hymn, "God of our fathers, known
of old," is sometimes sung in our churches, but it
was not written by an American. We are so poor
in national hymns, we have to go to Great Britain
to borrow one for our worship. We do not sing
often of our nation, because we do not have the
social vision.

Turn the pages of your hymn book and notice
how individualistic nearly all our hymns are. The
hymns that we like the best and that we sing with
greatest fervor are nearly all individualistic. Here
is a specimen from the 18th century, written by
Philip Doddridge:

> "O, happy day, that fixed my choice
>   On Thee, My Savior, and my God!
> Well may this glowing heart rejoice,
>   And tell its raptures all abroad.

> "Happy day, happy day,
> When Jesus washed my sins away!
> He taught me how to watch and pray,
> And live rejoicing every day;
> Happy day, happy day,
> When Jesus washed my sins away!"

It is a beautiful hymn. We ought to sing it. It
has a right to a place in the hymn book, but you
will observe that there is in it no reference to Judah,

no thought of Jerusalem. The whole hymn circles around my own heart and its relation to Jesus Christ.

And now pick out a representative hymn of the 19th century. There is probably no hymn more characteristic of 19th century Christianity than the hymn of John Henry Newman, "Lead, kindly Light, amid the encircling gloom." You will observe that it is just as individualistic as the hymn of Doddridge. "Lead, kindly Light, amid the encircling gloom, lead Thou *me* on." Notice the first personal pronoun always. "The night is dark, and *I* am far from home; lead thou *me* on. Keep thou *my* feet; *I* do not ask to see the distant scene—one step enough for *me*." That is the tone of the hymn all the way through, until at last you come to the vision of "Those angel faces smile, Which I have loved long since, and lost awhile." I do not criticize the hymn. It is a good hymn to sing, but you will observe that there is no thought of Judah, no glance in the direction of Jerusalem.

These are only samples of a great collection of hymns, some of which already come into your mind; for instance, "Jesus Lover of my soul," and "Just as I am without one plea," and "Nearer, my God, to Thee, nearer to Thee," "When I can read my title clear." These are only a few of the great host of hymns that our heart loves. Here are some others, "My Jesus I love Thee," "I am trusting Thee, Lord Jesus," "I lay my sins on Jesus," "I need

Thee every hour," "I've found a Friend; O such a Friend." In not one of these is there any reference to Judah, any allusion to Jerusalem. As Christians we do not have the social vision.

I am calling attention to this interesting fact, for the reason that it throws light on certain phenomena which have undoubtedly puzzled us. One of the outstanding phenomena of our day is the criticism of the Christian church. It is constant, and it is widespread. The criticism does not come from the foul mouths of godless blasphemers, but from many of the best people in the community—men and women of education and culture—of high intelligence and noble purpose. One often hears people saying that the church is asleep. That is a mild and gentle thing to say. If a critic has a gracious tongue, that is what he always says, "The church is asleep." But if a critic is somewhat rougher in his criticism, he says that the church is narrow and bigoted, or the church is wrapped up in its little creed, or the church is engaged in denominational bickerings and controversies. There are critics who go further than this. They say the church is filled with hypocrites—people who say one thing and do another thing. Now, most of us would never agree that these criticisms are accurate or just. We are acquainted with thousands of Christians, and certainly they are not sleepy. They are just as wideawake as any set of people in the world. We cannot agree that Christians are narrow and bigoted. There are a few bigots here and there, but a bigot always attracts attention, because he is a rare bird. There are not many Christian bigots yet alive. And as for Christians being hypocrites, that is malicious slander. It is absurd to think that the Church of Christ is made up of conscious rogues and liars, men and women who are playing a sham, saying one thing and believing another. Why then, are all these hard things said about the church? Why do men and women, ordinarily fair-minded in passing judgment on other matters, indulge in such wholesale condemnation when they come to deal with the Christian Church? I think it is because the world is in such a deplorable plight. Everybody concedes that the world is in a lamentable condition, and it is difficult to account for this when one remembers how many Christians there are upon this planet.

The statisticians tell us that there are now 556,-000,000 Christians in the world, and with all these hundreds of millions consecrated to the Son of God, how did the world ever get into such a mess as it is in, and why does it not get out of it? We have a Christian nation. There are scores of millions of church members in our country. Our churches are large and rich and influential, and yet what a plight the United States is in. The experts have been placarding the record which we made in the year 1924. What a dismal and heart-breaking record it is. In that one year $100,000,000 was stolen in forgeries. $2,500,000,000 was stolen in hold-ups. $6,000,000,000 was stolen in swindling stock operations. This is a part of the story on the financial side, but think of the thousands and thousands and thousands of murders; of the thousands, and thousands and thousands of divorces; of the thousands and thousands and thousands of culprits who stood in our juvenile courts. Certainly this is a record to make the heart sick. Dr. Russell H. Conwell, who has been all his life an optimist, always persisting in looking on the bright side of things, said on his eighty-second birthday, "I believe that American morals are worse than they have ever been to my knowledge." Now, when we have all these millions of Christians and find the country full of vice and crime, it is not surprising that some people say the church must be asleep, or the church must be attending to something else, or the church must be a sham and a fake.

I shall never forget an experience I had a few years ago when I was visiting a ministerial friend in a western city. At the dinner table he told me how prosperous Christianity was in that city, and how large and successful the churches all were, what good congregations they had, and what great contributions they made to missions and philanthropic causes. I was delighted to listen to so cheering a story. Later on in the evening we began to talk about the city in general, and my friend at once began to paint a picture black as night. Everything in the city seemed to be wrong. The Mayor was an incompetent and low-grade politician. The Board of Aldermen was made up of men totally unfit for the office. The courts were in a demoralized condition, and society was honeycombed with immorality and every kind of corruption. I was greatly impressed by the contrast between the prosperity of the churches and the wickedness of the city. Wickedness and worship seemed to thrive side by side. There seemed to be no point of contact between the life of the church and the life of the city. I could easily understand why critics in that city might say that the church is asleep, or the church is attending to other matters, or the church is a fraud.

Not long ago there appeared in one of the highest magazines of our country, an article entitled, "Can Christianity Survive?" I was struck at once by the radicalness of the title. We are accustomed to read articles on, "Can the Pulpit Survive?" To many people the answer is easy. It is almost axiomatic in many quarters that the pulpit cannot survive—it is already decadent and on the way to extinction. Sometimes the question is put thus: "Can the Church Survive?" and many persons are swift to answer "No." They believe that the church is obsolescent, and that it is destined for the scrap heap. Humanity is going to leave it behind. It is not often, however, that you find a writer discussing the question, "Can Christianity Survive?" I was all the more surprised to see such a title, because I had only recently been reading the church statistics of the last ten years. Many persons do not realize what rapid advances the church in this country is making. Whenever you hear people talking as though the church is losing members, and also ceasing to function in the life of the people, you may rest assured you are listening to persons who need information. The church membership is growing all the time, and the benevolent and missionary enterprises are increasing year by year, and the activity of the churches has never been so intense as it is now. When you compare the church of our day with the church twenty or thirty years ago, you must be astonished at the enormous strides forward which the church has been making. I have just been reading how many millions of Methodists there are and millions of Baptists, and millions of Lutherans, and millions of Presbyterians, and millions of Roman Catholics. I have read that there are over a million members of the Church of the Disciples, and over a million Episcopalians, and hundreds of thousands of a dozen other denominations. Coming fresh from these statistics I was somewhat startled to find in one of our highest magazines a sober discussion of the question, "Can Christianity Survive?" The writer began by confessing that he is not so radical as some. For instance, Mr. Bertrand Russell believes that religion cannot survive. This writer is sure that religion can survive, but he wants to discuss the question, "Whether Christianity can Survive." One of his first assertions was that

Christianity is not at present a vital factor in our civilization, and that Christianity is no longer reckoned with in the more complex problems and the wider social relationships in which the destiny of our civilization is being determined. I found the writer to be a man of intelligence and learning, a keen observer of the life of our generation, a man who had at his command a great array of facts, and I asked myself how can this be? How can a man of intelligence and information discuss a question like this, while at the same time churches are making amazing advances in every department of church life and work?

The only answer I could think of was one which I have already given. It is the impotency of the church in the presence of modern day problems that drives men to ask, "Can Christianity Survive?" The question was coming to the front before the war, but the war pushed it upon the vision of wider circles of thinkers. The Great War demonstrated that something was wrong. The Christian Church did not prevent that war. The question is, "Why did it not?" That war started in Europe, the oldest of all the Christian continents. The church is mighty in Europe. There are 375,000,000 Christians on that continent, and 90,000,000 of those are Protestants. There are three great hierarchies of ministers and priests, the Roman Catholic hierarchy, the Greek Catholic hierarchy, and the Protestant hierarchy, thousands and tens of thousands of ministers and priests, all of them educated, all of them consecrated to the Prince of Peace, and under these hierarchies hundreds of millions of professing Christians consecrated to brotherliness and service, and yet in the presence of this mighty host dedicated to love, a whole continent slips down into hell! There is something wrong somewhere, and no Christian should allow himself to get away from the problem which that war has presented. Not only did the church fail to prevent the war, but it did nothing to alleviate the horrors of the war. The war would not have been more horrible than it was if there had been no church at all. Men did their utmost in the way of cruelty and atrocity. They whipped the horses of science into a faster trot, that they might carry mankind on to new exploits of horror. It was one of the beastliest and ghastliest wars ever waged, so fierce and so inhuman that the non-Christian peoples of Asia looked on with amazement, and even the barbarians of Central Africa listened to the tale of atrocities, and wondered. There is something wrong somewhere. No thoughtful Christian should allow his eyes to wander from the problem which the war has presented. The Christian Church did not shorten the war by so much as a day. It would not have been longer if there had been no church at all. The carnage was not shortened because of anything which the church did or said. The war was brought to an end solely through the physical exhaustion of Germany. All the nations in the fall of 1918 still had the will to fight. The spirit was willing, but the flesh was weak, and because the body of Germany crumpled, the war came to an end. Here, then, we had a demonstration in the sight of the whole world of the impotency of the Church of Jesus Christ. The problem becomes all the more vivid and baffling, because during the fifty years before the war began, Christianity in Europe had been prosperous. Millions of Roman Catholics had gone right on from year to year, making the sign of the cross, sprinkling themselves with holy water, saying their Ave Marias and their Pater Nosters, and thousands of priests had celebrated millions of masses, offering up a daily sacrifice to God through Christ, and millions of Protestants had said their prayers, and had sung hymns no different from the hymns which we often sing:

"Peace, perfect peace, in this dark world of sin,
  The blood of Jesus whispers peace within."

And yet notwithstanding all this worship, the whole continent of Europe slid down into an abyss of blood and tears. There is something wrong somewhere. It is high time we were finding out where it is. "Can Christianity Survive?" It seems to me the answer is easy. It cannot survive in its present form. Christianity of the present type has not saved the world, is not saving it, and never can save it. The present type of Christians must unfold into a type that is more Christian. We must

[55]

get out of our individualism and gain the social vision. Without the social vision we never can have a social conscience. Without a social conscience we can never save the world.

We make a vast distinction between public sins and private sins. We judge men by the standard of individualist ethics. We condemn a man if he is addicted to vices that mar individual life. A man feels he is a good man if he does not drink or swear or gamble or commit adultery or refuse to pay his debts. His wife stands by his side, saying, "He is indeed a good man, for he does none of the things which bad men do." His neighbors say to one another, "He is a good man, for he reads the Bible, and he goes to church nearly every Sunday." But he does not think of Jerusalem! He has no interest in Judah! His neighbors do not measure him by the standards of social ethics, nor does he measure himself by such standards, and the result is that public sins abound. Let me remind you of two of them. Ellis Island has for generations been a public sin. It is the front door of America. Through that door nearly all the men, women and children intending to become citizens of our country come in. We have provided a vestibule there in which it is necessary for them to stand for a little while before we permit them to enter. It goes without saying that that vestibule ought to be beautiful and spacious and clean. It is important that we should make a favorable and wholesome impression upon all our future citizens. We are a rich nation. We have more than half of all the gold in the world. Our wealth has reached fabulous proportions, and therefore we ought to have provided buildings on Ellis Island, ample for their purposes. The buildings should have been the best that our architects could devise, or that our builders could build. They should have been provided with every convenience, if not with every comfort. All the officers and attendants on Ellis Island ought to have been men and women of fine breeding, high ideals, courteous manners and soft voices. But, alas, what has Ellis Island been in all these years but a scandal and a disgrace—a stench in the nostrils of the whole world. In America we have scores of millions of followers of Jesus who are consecrated to the service of "the first true gentleman who ever lived," and yet all these millions of Christians have allowed that scandal to go on year after year and decade after decade, until by and by the situation became intolerable, and it was necessary for Great Britain to offer a protest. The move was carried out in a most diplomatic manner. She made use of one of the most gracious and winsome of all her public servants. He visited Ellis Island, used his eyes and ears and nose, and sent in his report to Downing Street. His report was written with great restraint and was delicately worded, a constant effort being made not to irritate or offend more than was absolutely necessary. Congress took the hint and provided a small sum of money in order that Ellis Island might be cleaned up and new accommodations provided. Oh, the pity of it! The shame of it—that our Republic should wait until nudged by a Christian neighbor across the ocean to be decent in our treatment of immigrants! What is the explanation of this? There is no explanation except that we have little social vision. We are individualists in religion, and we do not carry our religion into the affairs of Judah and Jerusalem.

One other illustration: We are having great difficulty in enforcing the Volstead Act. Tens of thousands of Americans break the law, and not a few of these are members of Christian Churches. It is not simply ignorant foreigners in our great cities who are trampling upon the law, it is men and women in our highest American homes—men and women of culture and great social influence who openly deride and trample on the law of their country. How can you account for that? There is no explanation but this: These people have been brought up in the individualist school of ethics. They argue in this manner: "Alcohol does not hurt me, and therefore I propose to drink whenever I please." They do not think of Judah. They have no thought of Jerusalem. "Alcohol does not hurt me. I think of myself first. I think of myself last. I think of myself all the time. I do not think of anybody else but myself." Oh, the pity of it—that we have members of the Christian Church who have no social vision, and therefore no social conscience, and who therefore begin and end with themselves.

There is no hope for us unless we come up and accept the religion of Jesus. People sometimes talk of the "Old Gospel." That is the very Gospel I am speaking about. The "Old Gospel" is the "Social Gospel." Sometimes they speak admiringly of the Simple Gospel. That is indeed the Gospel that we all want. The Simple Gospel is the Social Gospel. This individualist Gospel is no gospel at all. Dip down into the teaching of Jesus anywhere you please, and you will find him preaching the social Gospel. "If you are bringing your gift to the altar, and remember that your brother has anything against you, leave your gift before the altar, go and be reconciled to your brother, and then come and offer your gift"; that is, social relationships come before worship. You cannot truly worship God until your social relationships are right. Your worship of God is meaningless and offensive until you are in right relations with your neighbors. That is the Simple Gospel. That is the Old Gospel. We must come up to it in order to be saved. Or, take this: "Go and learn what this means: 'I desire mercy, and not sacrifice.'" The religious people of Palestine criticized Jesus because he ate with publicans and sinners. They thought it was not nice. His action filled them with disgust. They were good people measured by the standards of their circle. They pretended to revere the Scriptures. They read them

often. He told them to go and read them again
and find out the meaning of a simple sentence like
this—some thing that had been written in the 8th
century—something that Hosea had said—something that Hosea had put into the mouth of God:
"I desire mercy. I desire humane, social relationships rather than worship." That is the Simple
Gospel—that is the Old Gospel, and we must come
up to it or we are lost. Or, take this: When a man
asked Jesus to name the great commandment, Jesus
replied, "Thou shalt love the Lord thy God with
all thy heart, and with all thy soul, and with all
thy mind, and with all thy strength. The second is
this, Thou shalt love thy neighbor as thyself." The
man to whom he was speaking, wore on his fore-
head a little leather box, in which he carried the
first commandment, "Love God." He carried a
similar leather box on his left arm. In that box
also he carried the first commandment. Jesus said
to him, "You must put into your little box, 'Love
thy neighbor as thyself.'" Those two commandments go together. You cannot separate one from
the other. Upon these two everything worthwhile
hangs. That is the Simple Gospel. That is the
Old Gospel. We must come up to it, or we are
lost.

On the last night of his life in the upper chamber,
Jesus said, "A new commandment I give unto you,
that ye love one another, even as I have loved you.
By this shall all men know that ye are my disciples,

if you love one another." Here again the emphasis is on social relationships. Men are to know that Christians belong to Christ, not by the form of their worship, or by the phrases of their creed, or by the form of their church government, they are to prove their Christian discipleship by their relations to men. That is the Simple Gospel. That is the Old Gospel, and without that Gospel we cannot be saved.

IV

A HOLY AND REASONING GOD

Let us begin with Isaiah's idea of God. A man's idea of God colors all his thinking and determines his attitude to life. The Book of Isaiah opens with the words, "The vision of Isaiah the son of Amoz, which he saw concerning Judah and Jerusalem," and judging from what immediately follows, the first thing which the young man saw about his nation and his city, was their wickedness. In the first paragraph of the first chapter we read this lamentation: "Ah sinful nation, a people laden with iniquity, a seed of evil-doers, children that deal corruptly; they have forsaken Jehovah, they have despised the Holy One of Israel, they are estranged and gone backward!" And then he goes on in language still more vigorous: "The whole head is sick and the whole heart is faint. From the sole of the foot even unto the head there is no soundness in it; but wounds and bruises, and fresh stripes, and nobody has attended to them. They have not been closed up, neither softened with oil." In portraying the wickedness of his country, no man has ever surpassed Isaiah.

March 1, 1925.

When did he get his eyes for the first time on the wickedness of his people? When did their sinfulness first pierce his conscience? When did it first stab him awake? Probably in the year in which King Uzziah died. In the sixth chapter he uses these significant words: "In the year that King Uzziah died, I saw the Lord." It is not unlikely that it was in the year in which he saw the Lord, that he saw the sinfulness of his city and his country. The year in which King Uzziah died was an unforgetable year. Death is always an impressive event. As Byron says:

> "Oh, God! it is a fearful thing
> To see the human soul take wing
> In any shape, in any mood."

You are going down the street and you notice a big crowd in front of you. When you come up to it, they tell you that a man has been run over. You wait a moment or two and you hear some one saying, "He is dead!" You go away with a hushed heart. You do not know who the man is, but that word "dead" has left the heart awed. You are walking through a street, and on passing a certain house they are carrying out a little casket. It is the casket of a baby. You do not know who the baby is. You do not know its parents, nor do you ever expect to know them, and yet you pass on in silence. The breath of the mystery of death has touched your heart and made the world for a moment different. But death becomes enormously more impressive when it strikes down a man whom everybody knows. Do you remember how you felt when word came that Caruso was dead? He was a foreigner, an Italian, a singer. Some of us had heard him a few times. Many of us had never heard him at all, but when the word came that he was dead, the heart sighed, and the whole world seemed to be poorer. You have not forgotten how you felt when Harding died. Nor have you forgotten how you felt when the word came that McKinley was dead. I shall never forget the day on which the word came that Garfield was dead. I was a student in an Ohio college, and the great hush that fell upon the entire student body when the sad news came, made an impression which can never be effaced. Garfield was a son of Ohio, and in his death all the people of the State of Ohio felt personally bereaved. Men have told me how they felt when they heard that Lincoln was dead. The announcement pierced their heart like a sword, and it seemed as though a great darkness fell upon the land. Darkness fell upon Jerusalem when King Uzziah died. He was Uzziah the Great, the greatest king who had ruled in Palestine since Solomon. He had been on the throne for fifty years. He was mighty both in peace and in war. Throughout his reign he had by his wisdom and energy extended the prestige of his country, and now the great king is dead. Everybody is bowed down with grief.

No one is more deeply impressed than Isaiah. He is in the hero worshipping age. The very heavens seem to him to have fallen. We do not know the details of that day. We cannot say with confidence what Isaiah did. Probably he was in the funeral cortège, and went with it with solemnized heart to the place of burial. It may be with thousands of others, he passed through the room of the palace in which the dead king lay on the royal bier. It may be that he looked upon the dead face, and that he then slipped away from the crowd and went into the temple to think and to pray. While he was there in the temple something wonderful happened. He saw something more vividly than he had ever seen it before. His experience is written out in the sixth chapter of his book.

I want to translate that chapter for you this morning. It is poetry, and many persons cannot make either head or tail out of poetry. The story is told in highly imaginative language, and the language of the imagination is to many persons Greek. I am afraid that the average man when he sits down to this chapter, does not make much out of it. The chapter opens with a description of those curious creatures called "Seraphim," each one having six wings, two to cover his face with, two to cover his feet with, and two to fly with. It sounds for all the world like a fairy tale, and it has no more influence on a man's conduct than any other tale. I want to translate it into the language in which you do your thinking. I want to express it all in prose. I want to tear away the gorgeous symbolism of the Oriental mind, and put the story into the vernacular of New York City.

We must remember first of all that this is a spiritual experience. It is something that took place in a man's soul. If you had been in the temple on that day, you would have seen nothing which is described in this chapter. All you would have seen would have been the walls of the temple and a few priests, and a young man with sober eyes and a pensive face in a reverie. Isaiah was thinking, and when one is thinking he does not know where he is. He does not see the things immediately around him. He is in a mental world, the world of the mind. Isaiah has a vision of his country. He cannot get his country out of his mind. It is passing through a crisis, and the young man has dark forebodings. He wonders what is going to happen. The forces of disruption and revolution are always at work underneath the surface, and when the strong hand which has long held them in check grows cold in death, is is impossible to say what will happen. As Isaiah thinks of his country, he sees how far it has fallen from those glorious ideals which had been held up before it by Moses and David and other mighty men of the past. He meditates upon Jerusalem and thinks of its sordidness and selfishness, and of the injustices and cruelties which mar and stain its life. He broods over the corruptions of society, and wonders how

long the tragedy of a rotten social life can go on.
The whole head is indeed sick and the whole heart
is faint. In the whole body politic there is not a
spot that is sound. This is what he is thinking
about in the temple after the funeral of King
Uzziah.

After thinking a while about Jerusalem and its
sin, he turned instinctively to the other world. Having looked for a season upon the things which are
seen, he turned for relief to the things which are
not seen. We always do that. When this world
becomes unendurable, we think of another world.
Death predisposes us to do that. When death makes
this world dark, we turn toward the light of the
eternal world. When the earthly king dies, we
think spontaneously of the King who is Eternal,
and so did this young Jew turn away from the sordidness of the material world and fix his inner eyes
upon the glory of the world that is everlasting. He
is now in the world in which God reigns. The
highest orders of created intelligence swiftly obey
the divine will. Isaiah is no longer in the temple in
Jerusalem. He is in the real temple, the temple in
which God lives and reigns. Maud Muller, you remember, when she began to dream, found that the
narrow kitchen wall stretched away into stately halls.
And so it was with Isaiah. When he began to
dream of the ideal world in which God's will is done
perfectly, he found the narrow walls of the temple
of Solomon stretching farther and farther away,

until at last he was surrounded by the walls of a temple not made with hands, eternal in the heavens.

After brooding awhile upon the Eternal World, he begins to think about himself. Here are two worlds, before his mind—the actual world and the ideal world—the world of men and the world of God. Surely these two worlds ought to be brought closer together. Love of God ought to be infused into human society. The ideas of God ought to be built into human institutions. These pollutions and corruptions by which Jerusalem is disgraced ought to be swept away. A great work must be done, but who is going to do it? The young man begins to wish that he might do it. He begins to ask himself if he ought not to do it. He comes to feel at last that it is his duty to do it. He is being called. He is being called by God. That is the way God calls men. He calls them through the world's need. He does not call them by any articulate voice. There were no voices buzzing in this man's ears. There were no ghostlike forms flitting through the air. Everything is spiritual, and the voice that speaks, speaks within him. It comes out of the need of Jerusalem. God is speaking to him, and the form which the Divine Voice takes, is the need of Judah. God is always calling us through human need. An old man falls in the street. He is stunned and cannot get up. You rush at once to his assistance. Why do you do that? God calls you. He calls you through that man's need. When in 1861 the flag was fired on at Fort Sumter, the Union was in need, and through its need God called upon the men of the North to pick up the flag and see that it waved over an undivided country. And so today God is speaking to men through the needs of the world. We talk about young men being called to go as missionaries. How does God call them? Through the need of the non-Christian world. Young men hear about the terrific needs of these vast populations, and touched by those needs young men and young women say, "Here we are, send us." We speak about men being called to the ministry. How are they called? They are called by God. How does he call them? Through the needs of our great cities and our rural communities. Young men see the lamentable condition in which society is, and looking upon the social needs, their hearts are touched and they feel a divine call to preach the Gospel. So it was with Isaiah. Having seen Judah and Jerusalem in their awful need, he heard God calling him to work for him.

And now observe what happens. Isaiah becomes convicted of sin. His immediate reaction is a consciousness of unworthiness. He feels that he is not fit to undertake the great task. Who is he that he should speak for God? The very evil which he sees all around him is also in himself. How can he consistently denounce sin when his own nature is so sinful? What right has he to speak for the Almighty, when he is so much like the men to whom he is expected to speak? That is always the experience of everyone who is called to work for God. One never feels his inferiority until he comes into the presence of some one who is superior. We are never conscious of our dress so long as we are dressed like the people around us, but the moment we are ushered into the presence of some one who is dressed in finer taste, with greater elegance, then we become conscious of the shabbiness of our own apparel. We do not think about our language so long as we are talking like the people with whom we mingle, but some day we find ourselves in a company of men and women highly cultured who speak the English language with a felicity and grace which we have not mastered—who speak every word with fine precision, and we at once become conscious of the shabbiness and awkwardness of our own slovenly speech. We are not conscious of our incompetency so long as we are doing little things—easy things which our neighbors all are doing. But some day we are asked to fill a place with taxing obligations—a position which rolls upon us heavy responsibilities, and we at once become conscious of our weakness and say to ourselves, "I am afraid I cannot do it." The magnitude of the task begets in us a humility which we had not known before. We feel that we are as good as anybody. There is in our heart no consciousness of sin, but some day we find ourselves in the presence of someone who is our superior in all the gifts and graces of the Christian spirit—some one who lives on a higher level and who is moved by nobler motives —some one whose spirit has a finer texture, and at once we become conscious of our coarse and worldly heart. Just so it was with Simon Peter. There was a time when he was just as good as any other fisherman who did business on the Sea of Galilee, but one day he made the acquaintance of Jesus of Nazareth. He became his comrade. He heard Jesus speak, came to feel the texture of Jesus' mind, and he at once began to grow conscious of the difference between himself and his new friend. The closer he came to Jesus, the more conscious he was of his own coarseness and shortcomings, until by and by this consciousness became unendurable, and he cried out, "Go away from me, for I am a sinful man." Peter felt that he was a moral leper, quite unfit to remain in the company of this man of Galilee. Just so it was with Isaiah this day in the temple. "Woe is me for I am undone, because I am a man of unclean lips." The uncleanness of his own nature comes into consciousness on his lips. He cannot undertake the divine work.

This conviction of sin leads to his conversion. When he is overwhelmed by the sense of his unworthiness, he turns to God. That is what we mean by conversion. In the Old Testament you read the constant exhortation, "Turn, Oh, turn." Sometimes it is expressed this way, "Return to the Lord, Oh return." That is the Old Testament way of saying, "Be converted." Conversion is turning from sin to the Lord. Isaiah in his mood of humility and penitence, turns to the Lord. Without him he can do nothing. Surely so great a God can make a man fit to do his work. Surely there must be in the heart of God a fire hot enough to burn up the impurities in a young man's heart. Isaiah believes that God can make him fit to do his work. He asks God to do it, and God does it. Isaiah feels that he has been cleansed, and thereupon he consecrates himself to the great work of saving Judah and Jerusalem. All through this season which he has spent in the temple, he has heard down deep in his soul a voice saying, "Whom shall I send? Whom shall I send? Whom shall I send?" The voice seems to float out across the city, across the land. It is a call for volunteers: "Who will go? Who will go? Who will go?" The young man hears the voice again and again and again. Finally it becomes unendurable. He can hold out no longer. He surrenders. He gives himself up to God. His surrender is absolute: "Here I am, send me." And out of the temple Isaiah goes, to give the next forty years of his life to working for Judah and Jerusalem. The only way in which a man can work for God is to work for his country and his city.

And thus does Isaiah's experience throw light upon a problem that is often presented. We sometimes hear people saying that they want the old Gospel, the simple Gospel, and by that they mean the individualist Gospel—the individualist Gospel that deals primarily and solely with the individual. They do not believe in preaching that deals with Judah and Jerusalem. They want preaching that deals solely with the individual heart. They ask these questions: "Does not everything depend upon the conversion of the individual? Is not the progress of the church conditioned on the regeneration of the individual heart? Does not civilization after all rest upon the strength of the character of the individual man?" And to all those questions the answer is "Yes." Everything depends upon the individual. The individual must be convicted of sin. He must be converted. He must consecrate himself to God. But there is another question which must be considered. How can you convict him of sin? How can he be converted? How can he be built up in character? The answer is, only by getting a conviction of the need of Judah and Jerusalem. It is when a man comes to see the need of his country and his city, that he hears the call to become a better man. It is only when he finds himself face to face with a gigantic task, that he realizes his own unfitness and inadequacy, and it is only in working for Judah and Jerusalem that he builds himself up in those traits of character which make him an effective servant of the Lord. It is through the social vision that the individual comes to new life and power.

Isaiah went out of the temple that day with a new name for God in his heart. Isaiah has the distinction of having coined a new title for God. The new title is "The Holy One of Israel." That is a name that Isaiah loved. It occurs again and again in his book, thirty times in this one book, and only five times in all the rest of the Old Testament, once in Psalm 71, once in Psalm 78, once in Psalm 89. All three Psalms were written long after Isaiah's day. The Hebrew poets of later date, took a delight in quoting phrases of the great orator of the eighth century. The title occurs twice in the Book of Jeremiah, but Jeremiah lived one hundred years after Isaiah. His book contains expressions used in earlier days. To Isaiah, God was always the Holy one of Israel.

He was not original in using the expression "Holy One." God had been named that before Isaiah's day. To the Jews God had for centuries been holy. Indeed all of the gods of all of the surrounding nations were holy gods, but the word "Holy" in the earlier times had no ethical meaning. By "holy" men meant "separate." God was holy in the sense that he was separated from the world of men. There was a deep gulf fixed between him and them. He was holy in the sense that they could not approach him—that he was immeasurably above and beyond them, but Isaiah takes the old expression, widens it and deepens it, and pours into it an ethical content. God to him is not simply high and lifted up, but he is a God of character. He is the God of Purity and Cleanness. He is the God of Righteousness. Every prophet has his own word which he likes best to

[74]

apply to God. Amoz loved Justice, Hosea loved Kindness, and Isaiah loved Holiness. To Isaiah above all the prophets, God is the one who is holy; but he does not stop there. To Isaiah God is "The Holy One of Israel." God is the God of Isaiah's country. He always links his country and God together. He thinks of God in relation to his nation. He is not so narrow as to think that God belongs to Israel alone. He is not so bigoted as to imagine that God is Judah's exclusive possession. Isaiah knows that God is the God of the whole earth—that he is the God of Assyria and Egypt, as well as the God of Palestine, but he thinks of God as in living relation to the people of Judah. In this way he saves his idea of God from becoming vague. That is the danger against which we must always be on our guard. The name "God" has always a tendency to become an abstraction, an algebraic X without any power to move the heart, and therefore to mould the conduct. God does not become a living God to us until we think of him in relation to the life of our country and city.

I often think of the honest confession of the good, orthodox church member, who admitted that whenever he thought of God he thought of an oblong blur. Many a Christian if asked to make a confession would have to say that same thing. God is a great blur. He is not a being in living relations with our own country and time. When we repeat the Apostles Creed, we say, "I believe in God the Father Almighty, Maker of Heaven and earth." That is a beautiful thing to say, and we ought to say it with confidence and joy, but we ought now and then to say to ourselves, "I believe that he is the Maker of the Catskills and Adirondacks, of the Appalachians and the Rockies, of Mt. Washington and Pike's Peak and Mt. Shasta, of the Hudson and the Mississippi and the Columbia, of the Mississippi Valley, of the Grand Cañon of the Colorado River." God would mean more to us if we visualized him as the Maker of our own country, and while we believe that he is the God of all the nations of the earth, it would be well if frequently we thought of him as the God of the United States, the God of our own land. It would help us all if we formed the habit of thinking that our country must be God's servant. It must be God's messenger. It must be God's witness. It must reflect his glory. It must embody his character. Unless we link God with our nation, he is likely to be an oblong blur, having no power to move the feeling or to mould our character. He is the Holy One of the United States, and since he is the Holy One of our country, interested in us, planning for us, expecting high things of us, what must he think of our commercial corruption, our political vileness, and our social rottenness? It is only when we begin to think of him as the Holy One of our country, that we become conscious of the heinousness of our country's sin.

We ought to bring him still closer to our mind

and heart. We ought to think of him more frequently as the Holy One of New York City. He is the God of New York. He is interested in this City. He plans for it. He sympathizes with it. He wants to use it for the advancement of his plans. How crude we are as yet in thinking of God. Many of us think of him only in connection with the church. He is the God of the church, but he is not the God of the city. We do not think of him as having any connection with the Mayor's office or the Board of Aldermen, or the courts or the schools, or the offices or the shops. It is very difficult for us to think of him as being interested in our transit problem, in our political complications, in our business transactions. How well-nigh impossible it is to link him in our mind with the police force or with Wall Street, or with Tammany Hall, but if there be any God at all, he is interested in all these things, and he is related to them all. He is the God of New York City. He is in the City and is working here, and if we do not see him working on all days of the week and in all sections of our city's life, then we really do not have any God at all. He is the Holy One of New York, and if he be holy, what does he think of us? What does he think of the filth that oozes out of the books which we allow to be published. What does he think of the vulgarity and the profanity and the obscenity which flows out across the stage of our theaters. It is only when we think of God as being the God of our city that we become sensitive to the heinousness of our city's sins.

God to Isaiah, then, is a God of character, who is in living relations to his country and his city. He is a thinking God, a God who reasons. He not only thinks himself, but he wants his people to think. That is their first duty. They cannot get anywhere without thinking. The first indictment which he brings against Judah and Jerusalem, is that people do not think. "The ox knoweth his owner, and the ass his master's crib; but Israel doth not know, my people doth not consider." In other words, they do not use their head. He wants them to think with him. "Come now, let us reason together." Let us think this whole problem out. Let us consider every phase of the question, and see if we cannot arrive at some satisfactory conclusion. That is a great idea of Isaiah, that God is a thinker who sits on the throne of the universe, and that he has created a race of beings who are capable of thinking with him. That is a wholesome suggestion for our own time. There are people who have the notion that it is not necessary to think in religion. You may think in other things but not in religion. They do not believe in theology which means that they do not believe in thinking. A man's theology is what he thinks about religion. There are many people who think that theology is unnecessary. In religion you must not use your head. You must use your heart, but not your intellect. There are many who feel that to think is presumptuous. Who are you that you should dare to think about religion? You have no right to think about the Bible, or to think about the Creed. You must take the Bible as it is, and accept the Creed as it reads. You must not use your mind. There are some people who think that thinking is dangerous. You must be careful and not think too much. You must beware and not think beyond a certain point, for you might undermine your belief. If you persist in thinking you may destroy your faith. All such persons need to sit at the feet of Isaiah. He believed that God thinks, and that God wants his children to think, and that one of the curses of religion is thoughtlessness. It is because people do not think in religion that they fall into formalities and superstition. Isaiah represents God as saying, "Come now, let us reason together. Ask all the questions that you want to ask. Bring up all the objections that you can think of. Lay before me all of your doubts and skepticism." This is the way in which he talks to men, because he is their Father. The father who is wise is never domineering when he comes to deal with his children. He does not say, "I believe this, therefore you have got to believe it too. I say this is going to be done, and there will be no argument about it." The father who is wise says to his children, "Now let us reason together. Let us think this matter over. Let us see what conclusions we shall arrive at. We must consider it on every side. We must face the facts just as they are. We must consider every point, and then we shall arrive at conclusions which are sound."

I presume you have heard people now and then say that the God of the Old Testament is a barbarian. Some persons have gone so far as to say that he is a savage. The next time you hear any one speak after that fashion, ask him to read the first chapter of Isaiah. On that first page God is represented as a Father: "I have nourished and brought up children, and they have rebelled against me." God is a Father who invites his children to think over the problems of life with him. This is one of the things which he says: "Though your sins be as scarlet, they shall be as white as snow, though they be red like crimson, they shall be as wool." Just think of that being said seven hundred years before Jesus came. No wonder the church has always believed that God spoke to the fathers by divers portions and in divers manners, through the prophets.

V

RELIGION AND MORALITY

A man's idea of religion is determined by his idea
of God. Isaiah believed that God is a holy and a
rational being, and therefore he believed that religion must be moral, that it must issue in an ethical
life. Religion, he thought, must concern itself with
everyday behavior. It must show itself in righteous
conduct. It must express itself in social relationships. It must be represented in civic customs and
programs. It must be incarnated in national policy.
If religion does not permeate and dominate life, then
it is nothing but superstition and has no vital connection with the Creator of the World.

Morality is indispensable to religion. This is one
of Isaiah's most dynamic ideas. It burns in him
like a fire, and whenever it touches him you can
feel the heat of the man. He is not long in bringing this idea to your attention. In the 11th verse
of the first chapter of his book, he begins to tell you
what he feels about religion. The seven verses beginning with verse 11, are the classic expression of
his conviction. He is speaking for himself, and he

March 8, 1925.

is also speaking for God. He is absolutely sure that God and he think and feel in the same way in regard to this great matter. "What unto me is the multitude of your sacrifices?" saith Jehovah. "I have had enough of the burnt-offerings of rams, and the fat of fed beasts; and I delight not in the blood of bullocks, or of lambs, or of he-goats. When you come to appear before me, who hath required this at your hand, to trample my courts? Bring no more vain oblations; incense is an abomination unto me; new moon and sabbath, the calling of assemblies—I cannot away with iniquity and the solemn meeting." In other words, "I cannot endure wickedness and worship." "Your new moons and appointed feasts my soul hateth." Throughout the East the new moon was celebrated with an elaborate ritual. All the Semitic tribes celebrated the new moon, and had done it from immemorial antiquity. "Your new moons my soul hateth. They are a trouble unto me. I am weary of bearing them. And when ye spread forth your hands (Orientals stretch out their hands when they supplicate God) I will hide mine eyes from you; yea, when ye make many prayers, I will not hear. Your hands are full of blood. Wash you, make you clean; put away the evil of your doings from before mine eyes; cease to do evil; learn to do well; seek justice, make that your aim. Put a check upon the oppressor. Restrain the man who is working mischief. Judge the fatherless. Secure for them their rights. Plead for the widow. Stand up for the woman who has nobody to protect or defend her. In short, moralize your religion, and let your religion express itself in a holy and rational life."

This idea of religion was not original with Isaiah. It had been the prophetic idea of religion from the beginning. Amos was one of Isaiah's predecessors, and he expresses his idea in this way, "I hate and despise your feasts, and I will take no delight in your solemn assemblies. Yea, though you offer me your burnt-offerings and meal-offerings, I will not accept them, neither will I regard the peace-offerings of your fat beasts. Take away from me the noise of your songs, for I will not hear the melody of your viols. But let justice roll down as waters, and right-eousness as a mighty stream (Amos 5:21-24). Hosea was also a predecessor of Isaiah, and he puts his idea of religion in this way: "O Ephraim, what shall I do unto thee? O Judah, what shall I do unto thee? for your goodness is as a morning cloud, and as the dew that goeth early away. Therefore have I hewed them by the prophets; I have slain them by the words of my mouth: and thy judgments are as the light that goeth forth. For I desire goodness and not sacrifice, and the knowledge of God more than burnt-offerings (Hosea 6:4-6). Micah was a contemporary of Isaiah, and expressed his idea in this way: "Wherewith shall I come before Jehovah, and bow myself before the high God? Shall I come before him with burnt-offerings, with calves a year old? Will Jehovah be pleased with thousands of rams, or with ten thousands of rivers of oil? Shall I give my first-born for my transgression, the fruit of my body for the sin of my soul? He hath showed thee, O man, what is good; and what doth Jehovah require of thee, but to do justice, and to love kindness, and to walk humbly with thy God." (Micah 6:6-8). That was the tone in which all the prophets had spoken. Samuel was a prophet, and one of the gems that came from his lips was this, "To obey is better than sacrifice, and to hearken than the fat of rams."

The first great prophet of Israel was Moses. We do not think of him often as a prophet, but rather as a lawgiver. He was both. He was a lawgiver with the insight and zeal of a prophet. His great contribution to humanity was the decalogue. He wrote the decalogue, but he was convinced that he was expressing the ideas of God. When he wrote those ten commandments, he was speaking for the Eternal. The decalogue is a moral document. It has nothing in it about sacrifice or ceremonies. After the first three commandments concerning God, everything is directed to morality. Men are commanded concerning the sacredness of parenthood, and the sacredness of the Day of Rest, and the sacredness of life, and the sacredness of marriage, and the sacredness of property, and the sacredness of reputation, and the tremendous importance of controlling the movements and desires of the heart.

It was the Mosaic idea of religion which had been repeated by all the prophets, and which finds fresh expression on the lips of Isaiah, son of Amoz. Other men express it well, but no man has surpassed Isaiah's unforgettable phrase, "I cannot endure wickedness and worship."

There are in the world two types of religious mind, which may be called the priestly type and the prophetic type. The priestly type of religious mind puts the prime emphasis on worship. It takes delight in ceremonies. It stresses the importance of approaching God in the right way. It feels that without a liturgy, it is not possible to please Him. To a priest religion is always a tradition. It is something that has been handed down from the past. It is sacred because of its antiquity, and his supreme business is to keep the tradition unalloyed and hand it down to those who come after him. The eyes of the priest are, therefore, often toward the past. He is by nature conservative. He is seldom in favor of innovations or new departures. His place is at the altar. To him there is no religion without an altar. God cannot be pleased without sacrifices, and the sacrifices to be acceptable must be offered by the priest. That man has played an important part in the religious history of mankind. He has had a rôle to play in all the great religions. When he is a priest of the better sort, he does not deny the importance of morality. He believes in morality and teaches it, but he does not give it the first place. The first place he gives to worship. He cultivates religion on its ceremonial side.

Over against the priest stands the prophet. He is a man of a different type of mind. His mind puts the first emphasis on life. He is interested supremely in conduct. He takes delight in unfolding ideas, in holding up ideals. He is not so conservative as the priest. His eyes are often toward the future. He is thinking of generations yet unborn, and is preparing the way for them. He has a more difficult job than the priest. It is much easier to perform a ceremony before God than it is to live on a high level of moral action. The priest seldom gets into trouble. The prophet is always in trouble. He is always irritating, and sometimes exasperating men because he insists upon applying the principles of religion to their everyday life. The prophet does not ignore altogether the forms of religion, he concedes that they have a value, but he does not set them in the first place. He stresses conduct rather than ceremonies.

It is interesting to note how these two types of mind have been colliding all through the religious history of the world. Open your Old Testament, and see how again and again the priest and prophet come into conflict. Religion always has a tendency to become overdeveloped on its ceremonial side. The worshipping instincts in the human heart are deep-rooted, and in many lives are very active. Judaism always had a tendency to become increasingly ritualistic. The leaders of the Jewish Church had an irrepressible inclination to elaborate the forms of temple worship. One of the deadliest of all sins with which Judaism had to contend was the sin of formalism. To save religion from formalism was the supreme work of the prophet. He had to stand up and resist with all his might the popular disposition to make religion a matter solely of form. He was always trying to push formalism back and crowd it down and break its power, doing his utmost to convince the people that God wants more than anything else, a life lived in right relations to one's fellow men. The Old Testament prophets were ethical teachers, not teaching ethics alone, but always insisting that religion shall issue in conduct. They were moral reformers, striking at the vices and sins of their generation, and trying to lift their people to higher planes of thought and action. The priest was often jealous of the prophet. He looked upon the prophet as a dangerous man. He accused the prophet of underestimating the value of ceremony. To the priest a prophet is always a man to be watched.

An interesting illustration of the way in which the priest tried to safeguard the people against the mischievous influence of the prophet is seen in the 51st Psalm. That is a Psalm which we all love—one of the noblest ever written. It came out of the heart of a prophet. The emphasis is placed upon the condition of the heart. "Create in me a clean heart, O

God; and renew a right spirit within me. Cast me not away from thy presence; and take not thy holy Spirit from me." Near the end of the Psalm, the poet exclaims: "For thou delightest not in sacrifice; else would I give it. Thou hast no pleasure in burnt-offering. The sacrifices of God are a broken spirit. A broken and a contrite heart, O God, thou wilt not despise." That is written in the great style of the prophet, but is it not dangerous doctrine? If God does not delight in sacrifice, then why should the priest go on offering sacrifices? If He has no pleasure in burnt-offering, why should burnt-offerings be given a place in the temple ritual? Certainly such a Psalm as that must not be allowed to go forth unamended. It must be edited by the hand of a priest. It was edited in this way. Some man, whose name we do not know, tacked on to that beautiful Psalm, these five lines: "Do good in thy good pleasure unto Zion. Build thou the walls of Jerusalem. Then wilt thou delight in the sacrifices of righteousness, in burnt-offering and whole burnt-offering. Then will they offer bullocks upon thine altar." What an anticlimax! What a coming down there is! For a moment we are in the presence of a beautiful sacrifice, the sacrifice of a human heart that has surrendered itself to God, and then in the twinkling of an eye, we find ourselves before an altar on which a bullock is being roasted. The poem of the prophet has been marred by the addition of the priest.

When you pass into the New Testament, you find the conflict continued, not between two men, but between one man and a group of men. Jesus and the Pharisees were in everlasting antagonism to one another. The Pharisees represented the priestly side of religion. They were lovers of form. Every part of worship was sacred to them, and each ceremony had to be performed in a precise manner. They had all sorts of lustrations or washings. They observed multitudinous rules in regard to Sabbath observance. They fasted a certain number of times every week. They were careful to pay tithes of all they possessed. Nothing could induce them to absent themselves from any of the great church festivals. They were so intent upon the ceremonies of religion that many of them lost the spirit of religion. Jesus said to them one day, "Why don't you go and learn what this means? 'I desire mercy and not sacrifice.'" In other words, "Why do you not get the prophetic standpoint? Why do you not put the emphasis where the prophets put it?" On another occasion he said, "The Sabbath was made for man, and not man for the Sabbath. You must not put an institution ahead of man." One day he said, half in humor and half in scorn, "You men take tithes of the weeds that grow in your back yard. You are so absorbed in doing minor things that you pass over the weightier matters of the law." On another occasion he declared in indignation, "You make void the word of God by your tradition." And so Jesus always threw himself on the side of the prophets. He loved to quote them. Their sentences ran through his mind. The first sermon which he preached in the synagogue in Nazareth was based on a paragraph in Isaiah. It is an interesting fact that he never called himself a "priest," and it is equally interesting that nobody ever took him for a priest. He did not act, or think, or talk like a priest. When at Cæsarea Philippi he asked his Apostles what men were thinking about him, the reply was, "Some think you are John the Baptist, some Elijah, some Jeremiah, and others cannot make up their mind just which prophet you are, but they are all convinced that you are one of them. You stand in the prophetic succession." When he rode into the City of Jerusalem on Palm Sunday, and men asked one another what the cause of the commotion was, and who that man at the center of the throng was, the reply was, "This is Jesus the Prophet of Nazareth." It is an interesting fact that no Apostle ever called Jesus a priest. They kept their tongue off that word. There is only one writer in the New Testament that ever called Jesus a priest. That is the man who wrote the Letter to the Hebrews. He is very careful, however, to guard us against the idea that Jesus was a priest in the traditional sense. In the 7th chapter of the Letter you will find that he is very careful to warn you against supposing Jesus was a priest after the fashion of other priests. He was not a priest after the order of Aaron. In other words, he was not a priest after the order of priests in the Jewish Church. He was a priest after the order of Melchisedec. Melchisedec had no successors, and Jesus of Nazareth was that kind of a priest. The reason why this writer called Jesus a priest, was because he desired to comfort the hearts of the Jews who had become Christians. They were feeling lonely and confused. It seemed to them that all the props of religion had been knocked from under them. The temple was burned. The altar was in ashes. The beautiful Levitical service was no more. There was no priest, and there was no high priest. They felt that everything worth while had been taken away from them. They felt very much as a pious Roman Catholic would feel in our day if you took away the altar and mass and the priest and the Pope. The average Catholic would feel with all those abolished, there was little left of religion, and so the writer of the Letter to the Hebrews endeavors to comfort these Jewish Christians, reminding them that they had an altar. The altar was the cross. And they had a sacrifice. Jesus had been the sacrifice, and they did not need any other one. In him they had a priest—a high priest who had gone into the Holy of Holies to make intercession for them.

Paul never called Jesus Christ a priest. That, to him, would have been a desecration, and he never found room in the Christian Church for a priest. He had been brought up in the strictest party of the

[91]

Jewish Church. He had been a Pharisee of the Pharisees, but when he became a Christian, he knew that in the religion of Jesus there is no room for a priest. His great letter on the Christian Church is his Letter to the Ephesians, and when he makes a list of the officers of the Church, his list runs thus: "And he gave some to be Apostles, and some Prophets, and some Evangelists, and some Pastors, and some Teachers; for the perfecting of the saints, unto the work of ministering, unto the building up of the body of Christ" (Ephesians 4:11-12). In the last book of the New Testament, the whole priesthood in the traditional sense is swallowed up in a Christian democracy, and the writer declares triumphantly that, "He made us to be a Kingdom, to be priests unto God." All Christians constitute a body which, like a priest, stands between the world and the Eternal, interpreting the heart of humanity to Him.

One would have supposed that with the example of Jesus and his Apostles before us, it would never have been possible for the priest to get a footing in the Christian Church. Little by little, however, the priest made his way in, and in the course of a few hundred years, he succeeded in getting the whole church into his hands. Christianity, instead of being a prophetic religion, became a priestly religion. It is not difficult to understand how the transition came about. In the first place, all of the religions of the world had their priests. Judaism had always had its priests. There certainly cannot be anything bad, therefore, about a priest, for Judaism was ordained of God, and Judaism made constant use of the priesthood. If the Jewish priests had been ordained of God, why should there not be priests in the Christian Church? There had been an altar in the Jewish Church, why should there not be an altar in the Christian Church? Sacrifices had been offered in the Jewish Church, why should there not be sacrifices offered in the Christian Church? And so an altar was set up, and a sacrifice was offered. The body of Christ was offered in a bloodless sacrifice by an officiating priest. In this way the whole idea of New Testament religion was transformed, and the emphasis was shifted from morality to worship. When once the work of elaborating the forms of worship was well under way, it went on with increasing momentum. The Church called to its assistance all the arts—music, painting, sculpture, architecture, poetry—compelling each one to make its contribution to the worship of God. The result of it all was, that the Christian Church succeeded in creating the most elaborate and gorgeous ritual that the world has known. But while an increasing emphasis was being placed upon worship, a decreasing stress was placed upon conduct. The church became immoral. Large sections of the priesthood became ignorant and superstitious. So little attention was paid to social relations, that the time arrived when a man who wanted to be an extraordinarily good man, turned his back on his fellow men and went into a monastery, and a woman who wanted to be extraordinarily saintly, refused to marry or have children, and hid herself in a convent. In this way Christianity ceased to be what it had been at the beginning, and became a burden and a stumbling block.

To be sure, the prophetic spirit never entirely died out. All through the middle ages the Roman Catholic Church had its prophets. The priest never succeeded in banishing the prophet entirely. Now and then the priest developed into the prophet. John Wycliffe was a priest, but he was also a prophet. Savonarola was a priest, but he was likewise a prophet, one of the greatest of the prophets of the fifteenth century. Thomas à Kempis was a monk, but his emphasis was the emphasis of a prophet. In his "Imitation of Christ," he does not dwell upon the ceremonial side of religion, but deals almost entirely with the things of the spirit. We Protestants read his book hardly realizing that he was a Roman Catholic at all. We feel that he is one of our own. It is a mistake, therefore, for us to imagine that the Roman Catholic Church ever became totally corrupt, or that it ceased to ascribe any value to the moral life of men. There were multitudes of pious and spiritually minded Catholics who longed for the reformation of their church, and through the 15th century repeated efforts were made to put an end to the abuses and lift the life of the church to a higher level. But all of these efforts were in vain, the result being that in the 16th century a great body of Roman Catholics came out of the Catholic Church, and later on became known as "Protestants."

What is the difference between the Roman Catholic Church and the Protestant Church? That is a question which is often asked, and it is a question which we ought to know how to answer. Is not this the correct answer? The Roman Catholic Church puts the prime emphasis on worship, whereas the Protestant Church places the prime emphasis on conduct. A Roman Catholic pays an attention to the forms of worship which is entirely unknown in the average Protestant Church. The Roman Church devotes itself to the education of its children in forms of worship in a way which we Protestants have never adopted. The result is that when it comes to an observance of the forms of religion, the Catholics are far superior to us. They have a richer and more ornate and more elaborate worship, and their churches have greater congregations than ours. They have made a specialty of worship, and they have their reward. They do not ignore morality. They teach morality, and insist on the importance of it, but they do not put so much stress on morality as we do. For instance, I could belong to the Roman Catholic Church and be a wicked man. I would not be a good Catholic if I were wicked, but I would be a Catholic, and the Church would not put me out; but if I should deny the supremacy of the Pope, I should be put out at once. That church emphasizes externalities in a way in which we do not. The Roman Catholic Church does not acknowledge that I have any right to officiate at the celebration of the Lord's Supper. It does not say that I am not so good a man as a priest, or that I am not so learned as he. It says that I have no authority to officiate at the Lord's Supper. There are many men in New York City as good as Mayor Hylan, but Mayor Hylan can sign papers that nobody else can sign. He can sign them because he is the Mayor of the City and has been given authority to sign them. There are many men in the State of New York as good as Governor Smith, but there are many documents which he alone is permitted to sign. It is not a question of goodness, but a question of authority. There has never been a valid celebration of the Lord's Supper, according to the Roman Catholic idea, in the whole eighty-five years of the history of our Broadway Tabernacle Church, for the reason that we have never had a man as the pastor of the church who had received authority to celebrate the Lord's Supper from the hierarchy of the Roman Catholic Church. That church puts the emphasis upon form. It is not true, as some Roman Catholics have declared, that we Protestants do not value worship. We give it a high value. We have our forms of worship which are sacred and helpful to us. We have the two Sacraments of Baptism and the Lord's Supper. We have our wedding service and our funeral service and our Sunday services.

We know that forms are indispensable to religion, but we do not place the prime emphasis upon forms. We are more interested in ideas and ideals, and the application of these ideas and ideals to the social and political problems of the world.

But in the Protestant Church we have our priests and our prophets. There are many Protestants who put the emphasis where the Roman Catholics put it, and there are other Protestants who put the emphasis where Isaiah put it. In the Anglican Church there is a large and growing body of Christians who call themselves Anglo-Catholics. They put the chief stress upon worship. Ever since the days of John Henry Newman, they have exerted a powerful influence on the Anglican Communion, and nobody can say yet what the ultimate outcome is going to be. These Anglo-Catholics feel that worship is all-important, and that worship to be full-toned, and to convey the full blessing of God, must be after the forms that have come down to us from the medieval times. The same division runs through the Episcopal Church in our own country. There are Episcopalians who despise the word "Protestant." They feel insulted if anybody calls them "Protestants." They are often known as "High Churchmen." They put the supreme emphasis upon worship. Any other form of worship but their own form is exceedingly unsatisfactory to them. They do not feel at home in any other church than their own. No worship is really worship to them except after the form to which they have grown accustomed. They are so interested in worship that many of them forget to put emphasis upon life. They are so in love with their form of worship that they forget to cultivate the dispositions which Jesus loves. He said to his disciples in the upper chamber, "A new commandment I give unto you, that ye love one another even as I have loved you. By this shall all men know that ye are my disciples, that you love one another." In saying that, he declared that the badge of Christian discipleship is not any particular form of worship, but a particular form of life. We are to live in loving fellowship with one another, and if we do not do that, we have not come up to the test which our Lord himself has prescribed.

These two types of religious minds are found in all churches. You have found them in the circle of your own acquaintances. You know men and women who put the primary stress upon the ceremonial side of religion. They are very particular about keeping Sunday, very faithful in attending church service, quite punctilious about reading the Bible and saying their prayers, but you probably know some people of this type who are rather indifferent to ethical distinctions. They are not always particular about telling the truth. They do not hesitate at times to be unjust or even cruel. It hurts their conscience to do things on Sunday which many other people do, but it does not hurt their conscience to be indifferent to points of propriety or considerateness, sometimes even of justice and honor. They seem to be more or less color blind in the realm of ethical relations. You no doubt know other Christians who have a strange indifference to the forms of religion. They seem to be willing on Sunday to do anything which they do on other days. They are desultory in church attendance. It makes little difference to them whether they read the Bible every night or not. As for praying, they can dispense with that a whole week at a time. They come to the Lord's Supper occasionally, but it is not to them a means of grace. To them it is a form which means little. And yet some of these people have very keen eyes for moral distinctions. They are very careful in the use of their tongue. They shrink from doing anything that would hurt others. They are punctilious about speaking the truth. Their sense of honor is high. They seem insensible to the claims of the ceremonial side of religion, but on the ethical side they are alert and wide-awake.

But no matter where we place the emphasis, we all need to sit at the feet of Isaiah, and listen to him tell us again that God is not interested in the forms of worship, unless we put an end to our wickedness. Let us translate his language into the language of our own day. When he talks about "new moons and burnt-offerings and the fat of fed beasts, and the blood of bullocks, of lambs and he-goats," we feel we are listening to a foreign language. We must translate it into our everyday speech. What

God says to us is this: "I am not interested in your church attendance and your prayer meetings and your communion attendance unless you go farther. I care nothing for your missionary meetings and your missionary collections and your Bible classes, unless they carry you farther. I am weary of all these religious forms that you are observing, unless they assist you in living the kind of life which Jesus lived. All this worship counts for nothing, unless you look after the morality of your press, of your stage, of your books, of your city, and of your nation. Cease to do evil. Quit your meanness. Quit your lying. Quit your cheating. Quit your swearing. Quit your gambling. Quit your loafing. Quit your shirking. Quit your skinning out of your obligations. Learn to do right. Study the way of doing right. Experiment in doing right. Practice the art of doing right. Go to school in order to learn how to do right. Work for a degree in the school of Christ. Some of you young men and young women who are working for a degree, the degree of "B.A.," or the degree of "B.S.," or the degree of "M.A.," or the degree of "Ph.D." What does all your book learning amount to if you do not know how to do right? All your knowledge of science and philosophy and the languages is worthless to this world if you do not know how to do right. There is only one thing worth living for, and that is to hear the King say, "Well done." Cease to do evil. Learn to do well!

Isaiah expressed his idea of religion in graphic and unforgettable speech, but Jesus is a greater teacher of religion than Isaiah. Isaiah was an orator. Jesus was an artist. Jesus could paint pictures, and by means of his pictures he made his ideas vivid forever. He has given us his idea of religion in the Parable of the Good Samaritan. He has given us in that parable his estimate of the priest and the prophet. A certain man goes from Jerusalem to Jericho and falls among robbers who leave him bleeding and half dead. A priest comes along, looks at him, does nothing for him, and hurries on in order to perform a sacrifice in Jerusalem. He must be there at a certain hour. It is important that the sacrifice should be offered, far more important than that a dying man shall be rescued. By and by another man comes along. He is another kind of priest—a singing priest—a member of the tribe of Levi—a member of the Temple choir. He must sing a Psalm. It is important that it be sung at a certain hour. He has no time to help a dying man. By and by a Samaritan comes along—a man who worships with a mangled liturgy—a liturgy which has not been approved by the hierarchy in Jerusalem. That man has time to put his arms underneath the man who is dying, and Jesus says, "That is the kind of religion that I like. That is the religion I believe in."

There is one other sentence in the New Testament which should not be forgotten—a sentence written by James—the brother of our Lord. It is a sentence of great significance, because it was written by a man who lived under the same roof with Jesus for nearly thirty years. The sentence occurs near the end of the first chapter of his Letter: "Pure religion and undefiled before our God and Father is this, to visit the fatherless and widows in their affliction, and to keep oneself unspotted from the world." The word translated "religion" means "liturgy." What James says is this: "The genuine ritual of the Christian religion is doing good." He was convinced of that, because he had lived for nearly thirty years with Jesus.

VI

SIN AND RETRIBUTION

'A man's idea of sin is moulded and colored by his idea of God. If his idea of God is vague, his idea of sin is likely to be dim. Isaiah was very sure of God. He saw him with remarkable distinctness. He saw him to be Infinite Holiness, and because he saw him as holiness, he saw the heinousness of sin. No man has ever dealt with sin more vigorously or masterfully than this son of Amoz. Read in the 28th chapter how he scourges the religious leaders of his people. He spares no one. Read in the 5th chapter how he warns the sophistical philosophers of his country who play with ethical distinctions and call things by their wrong names, calling evil good and good evil, and bitter sweet and sweet bitter. Read in the 3d chapter, how he lashes the women of Jerusalem. He has no more mercy on women than he has on men. He knows that men are not the only sinners in society, and that if a nation goes down, its downfall is due in large measure to the women. Read in his first chapter how he denounces the princes, with their dishonest hangers-on, and the

March 15, 1925.

judges with their itching palms, and the greedy landowners with their hearts hard as millstones. No man has ever pictured sin more vividly or denounced it with intenser passion.

It is an important mission of a prophet to condemn sin. One of the greatest prophets—Micah—declared his mission in these words, "I am full of power by the Spirit of Jehovah to declare unto Jacob his transgression, and unto Israel his sin." The prophets saw the malignity of sin, its ugliness and its deadliness, and because of the clearness of their vision they abhorred it, and because they abhorred it, they condemned it and warned men against it, and begged them to depart from it. This is why the prophets were unpopular. Sin is always an unpopular subject. Indeed it is quite disagreeable. No one enjoys having his sins condemned. Thousands of men are not in church this morning, because they do not want to think about their sins. They know full well that if they should come to the House of Prayer, they would begin to think of some of the wrong things they are doing, and this is what they do not want to do. No one likes to be told of his folly. Every one resents a rebuke. No one enjoys reproof. No matter how conscious we may be of our folly and our shortcomings, we do not want to be reminded of them. But it is a part of the work of a prophet to reprove and rebuke. Only a man with a brave heart can ever be a true prophet. The experience of the prophets is told in a classic passage in the 11th chapter of the Letter to the Hebrews. The passage is all the more tragic because it is so accurate, and states faithfully all of the facts. "They suffered mockings, and if they went on they suffered bonds and imprisonment, and if they went on they lost their lives. They were stoned. They were sawn asunder. They were slain with the sword, or if they did not lose their lives, they died a living death. They were ostracized and exiled and driven out of society. They wandered about in sheepskins and in goatskins. They were destitute, afflicted, tormented. They roamed in desert places, and on the sides of mountains, and hid themselves in caves and in holes of the earth. The world was not worthy of them, but God allowed them to suffer all these things because he was thinking of the generations that were to follow, and he wanted them to have a better world to live in."

Jesus of Nazareth was familiar with the whole experience of the prophets of his people. When a boy he had read the story, and as a young man he had brooded over it often. He carried in the back of his mind the whole thrilling history. He said to his disciples, "Blessed are you when men shall revile you and persecute you, and say all manner of evil against you falsely for my sake, rejoice and be exceeding glad, for so persecuted they the prophets who were before you. Count it a great thing to take your place in the company of the men who suffered hard things for God." He took up the work of a prophet, and expected to get a prophet's reward. On the last Tuesday of his life, he looked into the faces of the crowd of men in Jerusalem, saying, "Woe unto you scribes and Pharisees, hypocrites! for ye build the sepulchres of the prophets, and garnish the tombs of the righteous, and say that if you had lived in the days of your fathers, you would not have done what they did, but by your words and your deeds, you are proving that you are the lineal descendants of the men who killed the prophets. Go on! Go on! and fill up the measure of your guilt. I am going to send you prophets and wise men and scribes, and some of them you will kill, and others you will scourge in your synagogues, and still others you will persecute from city to city, so that all the righteous blood that has been shed upon the earth from the righteous blood of Abel down to the blood of Zachariah, who was killed at the very altar, will come upon this generation." That was on Tuesday, and on Friday these men were gathered together, shouting at the prisoner who stood before Pontius Pilate, and shrieking, "Away with him! Away with him! Crucify him! Crucify him!" And so he was crucified. These men said to Caiaphas, the High Priest, that Jesus ought to be crucified because he said he was the Son of God, but they told Pontius Pilate he ought to be crucified because he said he was a king. The real reason why they longed for his death, was because he had condemned them for their sins. He had exposed their hypocrisies. He had reprimanded them for their selfishness. He had condemned them for their cruelty. He had driven the traders from the Temple. He had asked the leaders pointed questions which pierced like swords. He had asked them how they could hope to escape the condemnation of Gehenna. Jesus died upon the cross because he dared to tell men the truth about themselves.

When we come into the presence of the Hebrew prophets, we realize at once that we are in the presence of great and clear-eyed men. They are not quibblers, or pedants, narrow-minded bigots, but men with wonderful eyes which see to the very core of things, men who have a genius for expressing facts as they are. More nonsense has been spoken and written on the subject of sin than on any other subject. There is no other subject concerning which it is so easy for men to become befuddled. There is no other subject concerning which it is so difficult to keep from deceiving oneself and being deceived by others, and driven off into sophistical and shallow forms of thinking. These prophets were all clear-eyed. They saw sin as it is. They did not attempt to explain sin away. That has been a favorite trick from the beginning of the world to the present hour. They were doing it in the days of Isaiah, and they were doing it in the days of Jesus, and they are doing it in our generation; but "If a man says, he has no sin, he deceives himself, and the truth is not in him." That was the conviction of the Beloved Disciple, and that was the conviction of Isaiah, and also of all the prophets.

The prophets never tried to tone sin down. They never applied to it soft and extenuating words. They never called it "blunder," or "error," or "mistake." It is all that, but it is more. They never called it "defect," or "flaw," or "immaturity." They knew it was worse than that. They never called it "ignorance," or "goodness in the making," they were too sensible for that.

They never attempted to deal with it superficially. Every generation brings out its horde of quack doctors—men who have eyes incapable of looking below the surface. These quack doctors are always talking about the "system." The world is wretched because we have a wrong system. Usually it is the economic system which is at fault. If we could only get rid of the system, then the world would be all right. Others think that it is a faulty or belated machinery. If we could exchange some of the wheels for others, and put in some new belting here and there, we should get rid of the things that plague us, and glide peacefully onward in triumph. Others think it is defective legislation. If you would only be willing to write down another law, then the Kingdom of God would come. Others think it is defective education. If you would only put up another school, all of the tragedies which curse us would disappear. And so the quack doctors came with their salves, and liniments, and poultices, attempting to deal with sin as though it were an eruption on the skin, a sort of scarlet rash, an affliction of pimples. But the prophets brushed aside all the quack doctors and all their quack nostrums. They knew that sin is a cancer, an internal cancer, and that it is gnawing at the vitals of humanity, and that the only cure for it is God.

Because they saw the malignancy and deadliness of sin, they saw the inevitableness of retribution. They said plainly that God punishes sin. He punishes every sin, and he punishes sin awfully. Some of us are too squeamish to say that. We think that to say that is a reflection on God. We hesitate to say it because we think that we shall thereby contradict the truth that God is Love. But the Hebrew prophets were not afflicted by that form of sentimentalism. They had no theory about punishment. They did not speculate about it, they simply saw it. What is the use of speculation and theorizing about something that you see? When I was a boy, most religious people were tremendously interested in the subject of "Future Punishment." They meant punishment on the other side of death. It was an interesting subject to discuss. What is the nature of it, and what is the duration of it? Who was going to suffer it? All these questions were debated with great enthusiasm and success. Every one arrived at his own conclusions. The Hebrew prophets never engaged in any such pastime, they were not interested in the world on the other side of death, they knew nothing about that world. Future punishment had no concern for them. They were tremendously interested in the punishment that was being inflicted all around them. It was present punishment that interested them and gave them alarm and pain. These prophets saw that the universe is governed by law, and that in the spiritual realm there are direful consequences which follow the transgression of law.

Within the last hundred years the human race has come to see as it never saw before, how the whole universe is governed according to law. The universality of law is one of the great conceptions of modern science, and modern science has driven that conception into us until now everybody is possessed by it. We know that every atom is under law, and we know that Mira and Antares, and Betelgeuse, the very largest of all the stars that tremble in the depth of space, these also are under law. We now know that law is unchangeable. It has never been changed. It never will be changed. And we also know that law is inexorable. We are in the grip of it, and there is no escape from it. It matters nothing at all who we are, or what we think, we are in the grip of laws which are unchangeable and inescapable. Put your hand in the fire and your hand is burned. No matter who you are, no matter what you think, your hand is burned. If you do not want your hand burned, then you must keep it out of the fire. If you fall over a precipice, you go to the bottom, no matter how far down the bottom is.

It may be 20 feet, or 200 feet, or 2,000 feet, you go to the bottom, no matter who you are or what you think, you go to the bottom. If you do not want to fall to the bottom of the abyss, then do not play on the edge of a precipice. If you take poison of a certain kind, and enough of it, you die, no matter who you are or what you think. Law is universal, unchangeable, inexorable. That is the kind of universe we are living in. That is the kind of God who rules all things. We have come to see that with appalling distinctness in the realm of matter.

It is an amazing thing that thousands of years ago, there were men in Palestine who saw with equal clearness, that the spiritual world is under law which is universal, unchangeable and inexorable. They saw that there are laws for persons just as clearly as modern scientists see that there are laws for atoms. They saw that there are laws for human hearts just as clearly as modern scientists see that there are laws for stars. These Hebrew prophets said, if you sin you get burned, no matter who you are or what you think, you get burned. If you do not want to be burned, then do not sin. If you sin you fall, no matter who you are or what you think, you fall. In our day we hear men jocosely talking about falling upward. What imbecility that is. There is no such thing as falling upward. You never hear of a man falling from the pavement to the top of the Woolworth Building. You never hear of an automobile falling from the bank of the Hudson to the top of the Palisades. You know in the physical universe there is no such thing as falling upward. There is no such thing as falling upward in any universe. When a man sins he falls. He is not on his way to something better, he is on his way to something worse, he is on his way to destruction. Every sin is a fall, and every fall is downward. If you do not want to fall, do not sin. If you sin you die. "The soul that sinneth it shall die." "The wages of sin is death." The prophets saw that. They saw it with startling distinctness. Death is not an event, but a process. One dies little by little. If you sin you begin to die. Keep on sinning and you die more and more. There is a coldness that creeps over the heart. There is a paralysis that creeps little by little over the nerves of sensibility. There is a deadness that creeps gradually over the entire soul, until at last the divine life is extinguished. So taught the prophets. It became a proverb among the people who had been instructed by the prophets: "Fools make a mock at sin!" Only a fool makes light of sin! Remember that, young man! It may be you have a companion or a comrade who makes light of sin. Beware of him, no matter what kind of coat he wears, or how good an education he has received, or how clever he is in intellect, if he makes light of sin, write him down a fool. That is his correct name—"fool." Never think of him as being anything else than a fool. Remember that, young woman. It may be that you have an acquaintance, or a friend who is making light of sin. No matter how pretty her face, or how fascinating her personality, or how plausible her speech, write her down a fool. That is all she is—a fool. Never lose that word. That is Isaiah's word. He called even princes fools. That is the word of Jesus. He looked into men's faces who made light of sin, and called them fools. If you ever find yourself making light of sin, say to yourself, "I am a fool."

Isaiah painted retribution under two figures, both of them so terrible as to awe the heart. He says that sin brings about an atrophy of the senses of the soul. If men persist in sinning, they lose the power of seeing, and the power of hearing, and the power of understanding. In that wonderful 6th chapter in which he tells of his conversion to God, he makes use of language in the 9th and 10th verses which, when you first come upon it, is certain to startle you. He says that God told him to go out and proclaim his message, in order that men having ears should not hear, and having hearts should not understand. That is the Hebraic way of saying a thing. We would express it with more words, and with greater care to avoid misunderstanding. What Isaiah means to say is, that he saw quite early in his ministry that if men do not listen to the truth, they become incapable of accepting it. If men go on doing wrong, then they lose the power of perceiving moral distinctions. If they persist in doing things that are wrong, they lose the power of hearing spiritual voices. If they go farther and farther from God, they suffer fatty degeneration of the heart and become incapable of understanding the things which God wants them to know. Isaiah found that out in his dealing with men. He proclaimed the truth with great boldness and clearness, but his generation had persisted so long in sin that they became incapable of understanding the message that came from God. It is an interesting fact that in the 13th chapter of the Gospel according to Matthew, Jesus quotes these words of Isaiah, saying that his own experience had been the same as that of the ancient prophet. He found himself talking to men throughout Galilee and in Jerusalem who had continued so long in sin that their eyes had become blind, and their ears had become dull, and their hearts had become so stupid that they could not take in what he was saying. It is interesting also, that St. Paul when he goes to Rome and gathers around him a large company of Jews, endeavoring to tell them about Jesus, meets the same fate which had overtaken Isaiah and Jesus. He falls back on the words of Isaiah, written in the 9th and 10th verses of the 6th chapter, convinced that the Jews in Rome are like the Jews with whom Isaiah dealt over 700 years before. They had eyes but they could not see, ears but they could not hear, hearts but they could not understand. That is the awful retribution which overtakes a man who persists in doing wrong. Little by little he loses possession of the very faculties by which he might be saved.

But Isaiah's favorite figure is fire. There is nothing so active, so aggressive, so penetrating and so irresistible as fire. This is Isaiah's favorite image for retribution. You find him making use of it at the end of his first chapter. Possibly some of you never noticed it. Here is the verse, "And the strong shall be as tow." Everybody knows what happens to tow when it is put into flame. That is exactly what happens to a man's soul when he does wrong. His work is as a spark. There you get a touch of the poet and the orator. "His work is as a spark." In other words, the evil in what he does sets him on fire and burns him up. A sinner is consumed by the sins which he commits. Isaiah goes on to say, "They shall both burn together, and none shall quench them." In other words, if you sin you are burned. It is an inexorable law. The law cannot be changed, there is no escape. If you sin you are burned. If you will turn to chapter 5 and read verses 18 to 24, you will find a wonderfully vivid image. Isaiah had often seen a field on fire. In the dry season when the stubble and grass had become like tinder, he had seen how quickly the flames would lick it all up. That is the picture in his eyes when he says, "Therefore as the tongue of fire devoureth the stubble, and as the dry grass sinketh down in the flame, so their root shall be as rottenness, and their blossom shall go up as dust," or to put it in prose,

they shall be utterly consumed. In the 9th chapter
his imagery becomes still more vivid. Now he
makes use of a forest fire. The nation has gone on
from bad to worse, until lawlessness has taken com-
plete possession of the land. It is all one vast blazing anarchy. Isaiah had felt the heat of a forest fire,
and had heard the roar of it, and had been awed
by the destructiveness of it, and he sees in that an
image of the destructiveness of sin. "For wickedness burneth as the fire, it devoureth the briers;
yea, it kindleth in the thickets of the forest, and they
roll upward in a column of smoke. Through the
wrath of Jehovah of hosts is the land burnt up; and
the people are as the fuel of fire." In the view of
the prophet, God is a consuming fire, and a nation
that persists in its wickedness is burnt up like so
much fuel.

At the end of the 30th chapter occurs another of
his most striking images. He is thinking of Assyria, the greatest of the world powers. In the 8th
century Assyria was the Great Britain of Isaiah's
time. Assyria is wicked. She transgresses the law
of God, and therefore she will be burnt up. He
looks upon that vast empire as a huge pile of wood,
and God breathes upon it, and it goes up in smoke.
It all came out as Isaiah said. The mighty Assyrian
Empire went up in smoke. Nobody today buys a
ticket for Nineveh. Those who go in search of
Assyria search among piles of dust, and just so will
America perish if she does not repent and learn how

to obey the laws of the Eternal. We have had in our own day, terrific confirmation of Isaiah's teaching. Why did we have the Great War? Was it not because the statesmen and diplomats were blind? They were honest men, but they were blind. That is why we got into the ditch. Why did all Europe blaze? It was because the conditions which Europe had created set it on fire. Unless we repent we shall all perish. In chapter 33 Isaiah brings us back to Jerusalem. He tells us that in Jerusalem the sinners have begun to be afraid. The questions which they ask themselves again and again are, "Who among us can dwell with the devouring fire?" "Who among us can dwell with everlasting burnings"; that is to say, who among us can dwell with God? Who of us can dwell with a God who is a consuming fire? How can we survive in the presence of a God who hates iniquity, and who destroys men for their sins? Here then is one of Isaiah's greatest and most awe-inspiring conceptions. He tells of God's righteousness as a devouring flame that penetrates the world, burning up wickedness like so much chaff and stubble, destroying everything that works abomination and makes a lie.

But that is not the end of Isaiah's message. He will not close with a tone so severe as that. "Come now," he says on behalf of God, "and let us bring our reasoning to an end." "Though your sins be as scarlet, they shall be as white as snow. Though they be red like crimson, they shall be as wool." It is possible for men to repent. It is not God's desire that any one shall perish. Do not allow anybody ever to say in your presence that the Old Testament is a savage book, a book written by barbarians. The man who says that has never read the Prophets. They are the tenderest hearted men that ever lived. They saw the severity of God, but they also saw his mercy. Listen to these pleading questions: "Why do you spend your money on that which is not bread? Why do you labor for that which brings no satisfactions? Why do you hew out broken cisterns that can hold no water, when there is a fountain of water forever flowing? Why will you die? If you obey, you will eat the good of the land." That is the pleading voice of the prophets. Do not say that the New Testament is less severe than the Old Testament. That would prove that you do not know either of the Testaments. Jesus of Nazareth is not a bit less severe than the prophets. He is even more severe, and he is also even more tender. He says that the truth is a rock. If a man stumbles over it, he will be broken to pieces, and if it falls upon him, it will scatter him as dust. He warns men again and again to beware of the fire of Gehenna, but his great heart was infinitely tender. "Come unto me. Why will you not come to me? O Bethsaida! O Chorazin! O Capernaum! Why did you not come to me, O Jerusalem? How often would I have gathered your children together, but you would not. Behold, your house is left unto you desolate."   Is not this the last word of the Christian religion—"God so loved the world, that he gave his only begotten Son, that whosoever believeth on him should not perish, but have everlasting life"?

VII.

THE REMNANT

If there is any boy or girl in the congregation who is wondering what is meant by "Remnant," I must begin with an explanation of the meaning of that word. Every woman knows what a remnant is. It is a fragment of stuff which is left over after the rest of the stuff has been used. Every dry goods merchant knows what it is. It is a piece of goods which remains after the most of the goods has been sold. Isaiah was not interested in dry goods. He was interested only in people. When he uses the word "Remnant," he always refers to people. It is the people who are left over after the majority of the people have been taken away. To him the remnant is the remainder, the residue, the minority.

The idea of the remnant is one of the dominant ideas of Isaiah, and his doctrine of the remnant is the most original contribution which he made to the religious thought of the world. Of course, the word "Remnant" had been used before his day. You will find the word in the Book of Amos. Amos referred to a remnant, but it was a remnant made up

March 22, 1925.

of negligible survivors. To Amos the remnant consisted of a few scraps. It was something like the fragments of a sheep which the shepherd pulls out of the jaws of a lion—two legs perhaps, and a piece of an ear—scraps that are hardly worth thinking about. That is the only remnant which Amos saw at the end of the destruction of Samaria. But to Isaiah the remnant is of surpassing value. Indeed it is of supreme importance. In the remnant lies the hope of the future. It is by means of the remnant that God is going to establish his kingdom on earth.

Let us see now how Isaiah arrived at his idea of the remnant. He began in his thinking with the conviction that God is Infinite Holiness. He is Everlasting Righteousness. He is Eternal Purity. Since he is all this, he is against all unholiness and impurity. He is not against these feebly or spasmodically, but fiercely, implacably, everlastingly, and victoriously. He cannot allow unholiness and unrighteousness and impurity to abide in his presence. All unholiness will be destroyed. All unrighteousness will be blotted out. All uncleanliness will be burnt up. At this point the prophet faces a startling question. What will become of his country, because his country is not holy? And what will become of his city, for his city is not righteous, and what will become of his people, for his people are not pure? He dwells among a people of unclean lips. Will, then, God blot out his nation and city? That cannot be. What would become of God's people—the people in whom he desires to make a revelation of his character and will? And what will become of his promises, for his promises have been often repeated—promises of blessings and of ultimate victory? What will become of his purpose, for from eternity it has been his purpose to rear a family of children upon earth who shall bring forth fruit to his glory. This is Isaiah's solution of that problem. "A remnant will return. A minority will turn to God. The destruction will not be total. There will always be a few who will repent and be healed." Isaiah found an illustration of his idea in the woods. One day he saw an oak tree that had been cut down. It lay upon the ground. Only a stump was left. Out of the stump there had sprung up a shoot—a sprout—a sapling. The oak was destroyed, but the vitality of the oak survived. The oak was down, and yet the seed of the oak had come up. The oak had been laid low, but nevertheless the life of the oak existed in another form. It lived on in the sapling that had grown up out of the root. Just so, said Isaiah, it will be with the people of God. Most of them will be destroyed, but a remnant will survive. There will be a nucleus, a core, a residue, and out of that minority, God will fashion himself a people, and by means of that remnant he will establish his kingdom on earth. The purposes of God cannot be defeated by the sins of men. The promises of God cannot be made void by the rebellion of the majority. The future of the world belong to the remnant.

THE REMNANT

One of the most wonderful traits of the human mind, is that it will not acquiesce in the idea of total and final destruction. You cannot compel the imagination to settle down permanently in the region of gloom. Soon or late it will soar aloft and bathe itself in the fountains of light. You cannot shut up the human spirit permanently in the dungeon of despair. No matter how thick the walls or how strong the bolts and bars, soon or late the spirit will escape and take up its abode in the palace of hope. "Man never is but always to be blest." Imagine for a moment the continent of Europe in ruins. Picture to yourself all her cities in ashes, all her fields laid waste, all her art galleries and libraries and cathedrals piled up in huge heaps of junk, her vast population reduced to a few stragglers half fed and half naked. Look upon that picture, and what happens? The mind immediately begins to work to create a new Europe. The mind refuses to believe that Europe is irretrievably destroyed. The mind will not tolerate a map of the world with the continent of Europe a desert. No matter how nearly destroyed Europe may be, the mind inevitably goes to work to build Europe up again. Out of the remnant the mind reconstructs a new Europe upon the ashes of the old.

Within the last few years a number of books have been written portraying the destruction which would be wrought by the next world war should another world war come. The picture is an appalling one.

It is not altogether fanciful, for it is based upon incontrovertible scientific data. The experts are generally agreed that another world war of any duration would put an end to civilization as we know it. When you read a book of this character, the heart is awed and depressed by the horrors which are painted, but when you reach the end of the book, you are quite sure that you have not read about the end of the world. The last syllable of recorded time is not war. The human race will not be ended by war. There will always be a remnant and out of the remnant God will build a new race.

Two or three years ago when I was traveling through the devastated region of France, I was deeply impressed by two things—the first was the flowers. They were blooming everywhere, along the sides of the roads and in all of the fields, and down into the craters that had been made by the bursting of huge shells. Even in these craters flowers were blooming. Not one of them had ever heard of the war. The soil had been soaked with blood, and underneath the surface there were mouldering bones, but the flowers knew nothing of this. The flowers were just as radiant as the other flowers had been which had bloomed upon these fields before four hundred thousand French boys had here tasted death. The beauty of those flowers was impressive, but far more impressive were the faces of the people. They had known all about the war. They had gone through the fire, and they had been burned. They had gone through the flood, and the water had come up to their necks, and their hearts had been torn by the torture of four years of agony, but now there was a light in their faces. Their eyes were toward the future. They were the remnant of the France that is to be. In their heart was a magic wand, and by the waving of that wand villages were coming up out of the débris. New homes were being created. In the midst of the ruins, cities that had been shot to pieces were taking on something of their former strength and beauty. The human heart will not rest in a world of destruction.

Our Bible ends with a radiant dream, with a picture that is dazzling in its loveliness. The picture was painted by an exile on the Isle of Patmos, a little rocky island in the Aegean Sea. The whole world was dark. The Roman Empire was at its worst. She was a huge beast, and all nations were prostrate under her cruel feet. The stars of idealism had been extinguished, and brute forces ruled the world. The only light visible was the light made by the Christian Church. It was a little candlestick with seven branches, seven jets of flame, all of them burning feebly and fitfully in the tempest which was blowing across the world. It seemed sometimes as though these jets of flame must inevitably go out. Their light was feeble and flickering, but in that feeble light the exile on the Isle of Patmos could see the City of God coming. It was beautiful as a girl in her wedding dress, beautiful as a bunch of jewels of indescribable loveliness, and the City of God was going to rest on foundations laid on the earth. No matter how dark the sky or how desolate the earth, the human heart retains its faith in the remnant.

Let us see how the Prophet applied his belief to his own life, and also to the life of the city and nation. Many of us have good beliefs, but we do not apply them. We do not apply them to our own life, the consequence being that we lack both peace and joy and power, nor do we apply them to our city and nation, and therefore we do not contribute anything to the spiritual growth and triumph of our people. Isaiah believed in the remnant, and he showed his belief first of all in this way. He named his oldest boy "Shear-jashub," meaning "A remnant shall return." That was a curious custom of the ancient Hebrews, embodying their beliefs and hopes in the names of their children. Isaiah had supreme confidence in the remnant, and when his little boy was born, he gave to him a name which would symbolize his belief. Whenever he saw the little fellow he would be reminded of his hope that a remnant would return, and whenever he spoke his name, he would have in his ears the music of his conviction. When he saw the little chap at play, his heart would be lifted up and made to sing by being reminded by the boy's name of the certainty that a remnant would return. Possibly sometimes at night when the prophet was despondent and wondered if the dawn would ever come, he was comforted by listening to the breathing of the little boy. He could hear his breathing in the darkness, and his breathing seemed to say to him, "A remnant shall return."

In the 7th chapter we are told how on a certain day the prophet went forth to have a conversation with the king. He took the little boy with him. He wanted the king to look upon him. He desired the king to know how firm his own belief was and how he had coined it into a name which he had given to his son. By his belief he quieted and comforted his own heart. No matter how terrible the storm, tranquillity was indestructible because of his assurance that a remnant would return. One of the mottoes of his life, a motto which he has given to all succeeding generations was, "In quietness and confidence shall be your strength." He used his belief in the heartening of his city and in the saving of his nation. In order to understand how he did this, it is necessary for us to refresh our memory of a crowded page of history. Let us remember that that was back in the 8th century before Christ. In that century the two great continents of the earth were Asia and Africa. In our day Europe and America are the great continents. 2600 years ago Europe was barbaric and America was unknown. In our day the two great world powers are Great Britain and the United States. In Isaiah's day the two great world powers were Assyria and Egypt. Like other world powers, these two ancient world powers were envious and suspicious of each other. Like all world powers they were military powers expressing their strength in terms of military equipment. They were always prepared for war, and being prepared for war it was natural for them to fight. They fought each other again and again, and in fighting each other, they trampled upon other nations. Between Assyria on the north and Egypt on the south, there were a number of small kingdoms, each governed by a king, and these little kings like the big kings were envious and suspicious of one another, and often fought one another. It was a world of ententes and alliances, of leagues and confederations. Two kings would combine against a third king. Sometimes one group of kings would make war on another group. The little kings often threw themselves for protection upon one or the other of the world powers. There were in Jerusalem always two political parties, the Assyrian party and the Egyptian party. The Assyrian party was friendly to Assyria, believing that the political interests of Judah could best be served by Judah allying itself with Assyria. The Egyptian party on the other hand was friendly to Egypt, believing that only in an alliance with Egypt was there any security for Judah. It was between these two political parties that Isaiah lived and did his work.

In the days of Ahaz, Isaiah had endeavored to persuade the king not to become the vassal of Assyria, but Ahaz would not heed his word. Judah called in the assistance of Assyria, becoming the vassal of the Assyrian king. This continued through the reigns of several Assyrian monarchs, but when in 705 Sennacherib came to the Assyrian throne, a number of kings arose in insurrection, determined to throw off the Assyrian yoke. That threw many of the Jews into a fever of revolt. The Egyptian party gained the ascendency and under the pressure of this party, King Hezekiah decided to join in the uprising. It was an unwise step for him to take. Sennacherib was like his predecessor, Sargon, and Sargon had been like his predecessor, Shalmaneser, and Shalmaneser had been like his predecessor, Tiglath-pileser. They were all warlike monarchs, taking delight in conquest. All of them were without conscience and without pity. Their ambition was not to build up but to destroy. They trampled nations remorselessly under their feet. The army of Sennacherib soon reached Phœnicia, and one city after another went down. Sidon fell, Tyre fell, all of the Phœnician cities and towns fell before the resistless advance of the Assyrian cohorts. Philistia then suffered the same fate. Ashdod, Ashkelon, Ekron, one after another capitulated. The Egyptians by this time succeeded in bringing up their army, and the Philistine army, augmented by the Egyptian army, met Sennacherib's army at Eltekeh, and the combined armies went down. It was impossible to stand against the Assyrian host. Sennacherib now turned his attention to Judah. One Jewish city after another fell until forty-six cities had fallen. Scores of towns were destroyed. 200,000 men, women and children were carried off into captivity. Cattle and sheep, so numerous that they could not be counted, were seized as spoil. Hezekiah, seeing that his whole country was in danger of being blotted out, decided to surrender. Sennacherib had now reached Lachish, only 35 miles southwest of Jerusalem. In a few days Jerusalem would be in his power. Hezekiah sends a commission to him asking him what he wants, assuring him that he will pay whatever he demands. The demand was an exhorbitant one. There was nothing to do but to pay it. In order to pay it, it was necessary to strip the palace of its ivory thrones and its ivory couches. It was necessary also to strip the Temple of all its gold. Everything that was most valuable in Jerusalem was sent down to Lachish to appease the insatiable Assyrian King. But even now he was not satisfied. He demands the surrender of Jerusalem. A deputation is sent to Lachish to beg Sennacherib to have mercy. There is no mercy in his hard heart. The envoys return to Jerusalem in tears. Hezekiah, however, does not surrender the city, and so Sennacherib sends one of his chief officers, the Rabshakeh, who endeavors to induce the city of Jerusalem to surrender by trying two different tricks. In the first place, he boasts in the presence of the Jerusalem army and people, of the invincible might of his monarch. He truly represents him as

the greatest king on earth. He runs through a list
of the other kings whom he has defeated, and then
asks the question, "Where are they now?" "What
did their gods do for them?" He then asks the
question, "What will your king do?" "What can
your God do for Jerusalem?" But the army refused
to surrender. Thereupon the Rabshakeh tried a
new tack. He offered them bribes. He told them
if Jerusalem would surrender, then every man
should have his own vine and his own fig tree and his
own cistern of water. They would live in security
under the King of Assyria. But even then the city
refused to surrender. The Rabshakeh returned to
Sennacherib disappointed. The Assyrian King wrote
a letter to Hezekiah full of boasts and threats, and
the king laid the letter before Isaiah.

Let us at this point pause long enough to take
in the picture: A city utterly helpless and discon-
solate. The king is irresolute. His statesmen are
at their wits' end. The counsellors are in tears. The
army is impotent. The people are in panic. There
is no possible means of deliverance. Egypt was the
only ally, and Egypt has fallen. There is no one to
help. The destruction of Jerusalem is inevitable,
and what has Isaiah been doing through these
troubled days? He has been heartening the king,
and pouring new life into the people. He has been
saying every day that the Assyrian King will never
take Jerusalem. He expresses his belief in different
figures. In the 29th chapter he likens the Assyrian

army to chaff. The wind will blow it away. In chapter 37 he likens the Assyrian army to a huge beast, and he says that God will put a hook in its nose and lead it back. In chapter 10 he likens the army to a forest. He says it will be consumed, that the greatest trees will come down, and at the end of the day there will be so few trees left that a child can count them. Why is he able to predict the destruction of the Assyrian army? It is because of his confidence in God. God will protect Jerusalem. God will save Mount Zion. Just as a bird hovers over her nest protecting her young, so will God hover over the City of Jerusalem, and it shall not be destroyed. There is a picture of faith! Looking not at the things which are seen, but at the things which are not seen, enduring because he sees him who is invisible. "This is the victory that overcometh the world, even our faith." It is the men of faith who save mankind. Behold the power of one man. In one of the critical days of human history, if it had not been for Isaiah, Hezekiah would have yielded. Without Isaiah, Jerusalem would have gone down. One man by his courage can hold up a king. One man by his confidence can put life into ten thousand men.

We are studying this morning, one of the great days in the history of the world, and at the center of that day there stands the noble figure of one of the greatest men God ever made—Isaiah, the son of Amoz. It all came out just as the prophet said. Jerusalem was not taken. The beast had a hook put into his nose, and it was led back to the Valley of the Euphrates. The army of Sennacherib, like a great forest, took fire, and was reduced to ashes. Why was Jerusalem not taken? What happened to the army of Sennacherib? The Assyrian records are silent on that question. Ninety-five years ago, there was dug up in the ruins of Nineveh a cylinder on which is written the story of this whole campaign. The story is written in the first person by Sennacherib himself. He tells what he did: "I captured so many cities. I made captive so many thousands of people. I seized as spoil so many cattle and sheep. I shut up in Jerusalem the King like a bird in his cage," and then the story suddenly fails. We are not told why the city was not captured. We only know that Sennacherib returned home, and although he lived twenty years longer, he never came back to Judah again. He had learned his lesson. Herodotus, the Father of History, a Greek historian, who lived 250 years after Isaiah, records a tradition to the effect that Sennacherib's expedition failed, because a horde of field mice gnawed the strings of the bows of his soldiers. Herodotus had gotten this story from the monuments of the Egyptians. The Jewish explanation is given in the 19th chapter of the second Book of Kings, and also in the 37th chapter of the Book of Isaiah. "And the angel of Jehovah went forth, and smote in the camp of the Assyrians a hundred and fourscore and five thousand; and when men arose early in the morning, behold, these were all dead bodies." By "the angel of the Lord," the Hebrew historian meant some force in nature. All the forces of nature, according to Hebrew thinkers were messengers of God—"Stormy winds fulfilled his word." Just which force of nature was the Angel of the Lord in this particular instance, we do not know. It may have been a simoon —a sand storm which again and again has destroyed thousands of lives. It may be that the army ventured on the Serbonian bog which stretches out on the east of the eastern mouth of the Nile. That is one of the most treacherous of all bogs. When the dry sand is driven out across it, the bog takes on the appearance of solid land, and more than one army venturing out upon the deceitful surface, has found itself gradually sinking, only to be swallowed up. Most likely the flower of the Assyrian army was annihilated by a pestilence, a pestilence which may have been generated in the Serbonian bog. Deadly miasmas were always floating over the land from that bog, and in those early days when there was no medical science as yet, it was impossible to check a plague, and not infrequently men were swept off by the tens of thousands like so many flies. It is not at all unlikely that 185,000 Assyrian soldiers might have been swept away by a plague. We only know that something wonderful happened. We know that Jerusalem was not captured. We know that Sennacherib returned to Nineveh. Lord

Byron in one of the most musical of his poems has told us of the wonderful deliverance:

"The Assyrian came down like the wolf on the fold,
And his cohorts were gleaming in purple and gold;
And the sheen of their spears was like stars on the sea,
When the blue wave rolls nightly on deep Galilee.

And the widows of Ashur are loud in their wail,
And the idols are broke in the temple of Baal;
And the might of the Gentile, unsmote by the sword,
Hath melted like snow in the glance of the Lord."

Now, what shall all this mean for us? Of what use can the doctrine of the remnant be to us? In the first place, it can save us from cynicism. There is a spirit of cynicism abroad, and the cynicism is the result of our failure to believe in the remnant. You hear men constantly dealing in generalizations, making sweeping assertions which are not true. We have all heard statements like this: "All politicians are demagogues and partisans!" "All the labor leaders are robbers and ruffians!" "All the young people of our day are Bolsheviks and pleasure-seekers!" "All Orientals are tricky and crooked!" "All Christians are hypocrites and bigots!" When we make use of such sneering statements, we are on our way to cynicism. If all humanity have gone astray and are hopeless, then why should we go on and work? Why should we want to live? There was a Hebrew prophet who, in a fit of despondency, became a cynic. He said in his despair, "All of my countrymen have gone after Baal, all of them are materialists. All of them have bowed down to the sensual and the brutal." When he came to believe that, he lost his power to work. No man can do his work when his heart has lost faith in his fellows. Later on the prophet did not care to live. He wanted to die. Why should any one care to live when all his fellow men have proved untrue? The Hebrew prophet fortunately did not remain in his mood of cynicism. He came to see that there was a remnant—a minority, who were still true to God, and when that fact was made clear to him, he went back to work again, and life took on its former zest and gladness. Let us always believe in the remnant. Let us keep on saying to ourselves, and also to others, "*Some* politicians are not demagogues and partisans. *Some* labor leaders are men of conscience and good sense. *Some* young people are true to the old traditions, and can be counted on in our work for God. *Some* Orientals are men of high ideals, and men of noble purposes, and *some* Christians are loyal to Christ, and ready to sacrifice for the advancement of His Kingdom." It is in our belief in the remnant that we are able to live and labor.

We Americans, above all others, are in need of the doctrine of the remnant. We are living in a country where political issues are decided by majorities. There is danger of us concluding that moral issues are decided in the same way. We must beware of being dominated by majorities, or being misled by them. It is just as absurd to say that majorities are always right as it is to say that majorities are always wrong. A majority may be right, and a majority may be wrong. We must find out in each case why it is right or wrong. There is an adage that, "The voice of the people is the voice of God," but that is an adage which is false. It is absurd to say that the voice of the people is always the voice of God, and it is equally absurd to say that the voice of the people is never the voice of God. Sometimes it is the voice of God and sometimes it is the voice of the devil. People can be blinded by passion, twisted by prejudice, paralyzed by ignorance. Again and again people have trampled on the law of God. On a never-to-be-forgotten day the people of Jerusalem crowded around Pontius Pilate's court, looking with fury in their eyes upon a prisoner who stood there, and crying "Crucify him! Away with him! Crucify him!" He was the best man that had ever walked the earth, the man with the noblest mind, and the gentlest heart that this world had ever seen, but the people of Jerusalem cried, "Away with him! Crucify him!" The hope of America does not lie in the masses. The hope of America lies in the remnant. It is the little company of Americans of cultivated taste and sensitive conscience and high ideals who constitute our only hope for the future.

What is true of our nation is equally true of our city. We will not say that New York City is all right because it has six million inhabitants. There is no ground for rejoicing in that. You cannot look to the six millions of our people for guidance. It is not because we have six millions of people that we can face the future undaunted. It is in the remnant of New York that we find safety. New York would fall into chaos if it were not for the nucleus of God-fearing people who live here. It is only because we have a remnant of men and women, law-abiding and God-fearing that we dare to expect anything good in the future. In the 18th chapter of the old Book of Genesis, Abraham is represented as having a conversation with God in regard to the destruction of Sodom. God is represented as saying to Abraham, that he would save the city if there were fifty righteous men in it. He would save it if there were forty, or thirty, or twenty, or even ten. A very small remnant is sufficient to save a city from ruin. Let us believe that. Let us believe that New York City is saved because of its remnant of righteous men and women.

We need the same doctrine of the remnant when we think of the Christian Church. We are told that there are hundreds of millions of Christians. What of it? Is there anything to rejoice in because of that? What do hundreds of millions of these Christians amount to when it comes to doing the work of the Lord? We are reminded often that we have tens of millions of church members in this country. What of it? Will the country be saved by all these? No, the Church of Christ is to be saved by the remnant. It is by the little nucleus of men and women who have been baptized into the spirit of Jesus, and who are ready day by day to carry the cross, that the Christian Church is to become at last a glorious church without spot or wrinkle, or any such thing. The hope of the church lies in the remnant.

VIII

THE MESSIAH

The word "Messiah" is a Hebrew word. We have used it so long that it sounds like English, but it is not English, and we do well now and then to translate it into English. It means in English "The Anointed One." If you translate "Messiah" into Greek, you have "Christos," and if you translate it into Latin you have "Christus." If you translate the Greek or Latin into English, you have "Christ." The name of the Founder of the Christian Religion is Jesus Christ, which being interpreted means "Jesus, the Messiah," or "The Anointed One." Our subject this morning is a most fascinating one to all studious-minded Christians.

There were three classes of men among the ancient Hebrews, who were anointed with oil when they entered upon the duties of their high office— the Prophets, the Priests and the Kings. You remember that Elijah was told to anoint Elisha as his successor, and that God told Moses to anoint his brethren to serve as priests, and that Samuel, the Judge, anointed Saul, and later on David as King. A king became known as the "Lord's Anointed."

March 29, 1925.

The ceremony of anointing was always a solemnizing one, because it was sacramental. The oil was the visible sign of an invisible grace. A king was assumed to be the representative of God upon earth, and therefore he enjoyed an intimacy with God which other men did not possess. In order to fulfill his high office, he was in need of a special measure of divine grace. The Hebrew people believe that when a man was anointed king, he was at the same time anointed by the spirit of God, and so a king at his coronation was anointed in two ways: he was anointed by man with oil, and he was anointed by the Almighty with the Holy Spirit.

But all these anointed men were disappointing. They never came up to the highest expectations of the people. The actual king was always falling short of the ideal king. The prophets did not always prove to be reliable spokesmen of God. Now and then a false note stole into their message. Their vision was clouded, and they became blind leaders of the blind. The priest was supposed to be a holy man, but in many instances he became worldly and selfish and sometimes vile. A king ought to be wise and strong and noble, but kings often proved to be foolish and weak and wicked. They never came up to the dream of the heart.

Now the human mind is so constructed that it idealizes both the past and the future. We all do that instinctively. We idealize our childhood, and we also idealize the future. Every nation idealizes its early life, and every nation also idealizes the time that is coming. No nation probably ever was endowed more richly with the idealizing faculty than the Hebrew people. They placed the Garden of Eden in the far-distant past, and far in front of them they placed the City of God. They never allowed themselves to be daunted or overwhelmed by the present, no matter how dark and troubled it was. They were always saved by hope. It was when the skies were darkest that they saw most clearly a good time coming, and it was when the worst king sat on the throne that they saw most distinctly the face of the ideal king.

When the vision of the ideal king first slipped into the Hebrew mind, we do not know. We know that the prophets of the 9th century did not get their eye on the ideal king. There is nothing in the recorded words of Elijah or Elisha which indicates that such a dream had taken possession of their soul. We know that the prophets of the first half of the 8th century were also indifferent to the ideal king. The greatest of these prophets were Amos and Hosea, and neither one of them gives us a picture of the coming king. Amos gives us a vision of the golden age—the ideal kingdom, but he says nothing about the ideal king. In the 5th verse of the 3rd chapter of Hosea, the prophet makes a passing reference to the ideal king. He says the children of Israel will return and seek Jehovah their God and David their King. David had now been dead 250 years, and had become idealized as a glorious monarch. The Hebrews in the days of Hosea could think of no king more superb and more mighty than King David. Hosea, therefore, in picturing the future, thinks of the two kingdoms uniting again, seeking Jehovah their God and David their King. Not the former David, but another David, equally potent and wise, whom God would surely send. This is the only hint of an ideal ruler which we find in the prophets of the first half of the 8th century. It is not until we come to Isaiah, the son of Amoz, that we find a portrait of the ideal king. Isaiah does not call him the "Lord's Anointed," or the "Messiah." In one passage he calls him a "Son," in another passage he calls him a "Shoot," and in a third passage he calls him a "King." He does not speak of him often. He speaks often of the ideal kingdom, but seldom does he get his eyes on the ideal king.

From the days of Isaiah onward, the idea which he introduced into religious thought, became more and more prominent in Hebrew thinking. Through the 700 years between the days of Isaiah and the coming of Jesus, the Messianic idea was not long out of the Hebrew mind. Sometimes it came forward with remarkable brilliancy, and then it would fade and become dim, and at times disappeared altogether only to come back again with new majesty and force. The form of the idea was constantly changing, depending upon the conditions of the age.

Sometimes the Messiah was a king, and sometimes a judge, and sometimes a warrior, and sometimes a conqueror, and sometimes a servant, and sometimes a redeemer, and finally a Son of Man. The vision of the ideal ruler took shape under the pressure of the age. At first the image is rather vague, but little by little it becomes more clear-cut and vivid. It is clearer in the second Isaiah than in the first. It becomes still more distinct in Zechariah, and takes on a new clearness in Daniel. After the closing of the Old Testament canon, a form of literature sprang up in which the Messiah took an exceedingly prominent place. In the Sibylline Oracles, written about the middle of the second century, the Messiah is a distinct individual. He is still more mysterious and majestic in the Book of Enoch, which appeared probably near the close of the second century, B.C. He is still more distinct in the Psalms of Solomon which appeared about the middle of the first century before Christ. For 200 years before the coming of Jesus, the curiosity of the people had been whetted by apocalyptic writers. The imagination became feverish, and the whole nation stood, as it were, on tiptoe waiting for the expected Messiah.

You must keep all that history in your mind in order to understand many expressions in the New Testament. When John the Baptist appeared, one of the first things he said was, "Do not think that I am the Messiah. I am not the one you are expecting. I am not the bridegroom. I am just the friend of the bridegroom. I am not the coming king. I am nothing but a voice crying in the wilderness preparing the way of the Lord and making his paths straight." When Andrew had an interview with Jesus, he was so profoundly impressed by what he saw and heard, that he rushed immediately in search of his brother Simon, and when he found him, he exclaimed, "We have found the Messiah." We have often read those words half asleep, forgetting the fire that was in them when they were first spoken, and the thrill which they sent through Simon's soul. How widespread the expectation was can be seen from a remark of the woman of Samaria, with whom Jesus had a conversation at Jacob's well. Here was a poor ignorant woman belonging to a belated race, who nevertheless was expecting the Messiah. She said to Jesus, "I know that the Messiah is coming, and when he comes he will tell us everything." The New Testament tells us that when Jesus was talking to the Jews, he was again and again interrupted by men who fell into controversy concerning whom he was. Some said, "This must be the Messiah." Others shouted back, "He is not." Now and again they implored Jesus to tell them plainly whether or not he was the Messiah.

Let us now take up Isaiah's idea of the Messiah, I mean the idea expressed in the first thirty-nine chapters of the book which bears Isaiah's name. There are only three paragraphs in which we get a glimpse of the coming king. The first paragraph is the first seven verses of the 9th chapter. The second paragraph is the first five verses of the 11th chapter. The third paragraph is the first eight verses of the 32d chapter—20 verses in all. It is surprising that Isaiah has so little to say about the ideal king.

I presume some of you are wondering why I do not include in the list of Messianic passages the fourteenth verse of the 7th chapter. That is the most famous verse in the whole thirty-nine chapters of Isaiah. From the very earliest times, it has been counted distinctly Messianic, but modern scholarship has compelled us to revise that opinion. Through nineteen Christian centuries illustrious scholars of the Christian Church have found in the 14th verse of the 7th chapter of Isaiah, reference to the Virgin Birth of Jesus. "Therefore, the Lord himself will give you a sign: behold, a virgin shall conceive and bear a son, and shall call his name Immanuel." Christians have long loved to believe that 700 years before the advent of Jesus, a prophet saw his coming and also foretold the manner of his birth. But a closer study of the context has convinced impartial scholars that this verse contains no reference to Jesus of Nazareth or to the ideal king. There is no hint in this verse of a miraculous conception or of a Virgin Birth.

This is the conclusion of the Bible experts. You need not take their word for it. You can decide the matter for yourself. The facts are very few and also very clear, and the conclusion to be drawn is unescapable. Here is the situation. Two kings were going to make war on Judah—the king of Syria and the King of Israel—and the King of Judah was greatly alarmed. He felt he was a match for either king alone, but he dared not meet both of them combined. His people also were panic-stricken and their hearts were fluttering as leaves flutter on a tree when the wind blows. Isaiah, the Prophet, does not share this fear. He sees nothing to be alarmed at in the threatened invasion of these two kings. He decides to talk the matter over with King Ahaz. He begs the King not to be afraid. He calls the two belligerent kings, "The tails of smoking firebrands." He assures Ahaz that they will never be able to accomplish their purpose, and that in a short time these two kings will be down and out. Ahaz cannot be convinced. His heart continues to tremble, and he is fixed in his determination to throw himself on the protection of the Assyrian King. As a last resort, the prophet begs him to ask God for a sign. Ahaz refuses, whereupon the prophet says, "Therefore, the Lord himself will give you a sign: behold, a virgin shall conceive and bear a son, and shall call his name Immanuel." Mark well that the sign is to be given to Ahaz, and the sign is a child to be born soon. Now, if the prophet is referring to Jesus of Nazareth, he made a bad guess. The year in which he promised the sign was 734 B.C., and Jesus of Nazareth was born 730 years later. How could Jesus of Nazareth be a sign to Ahaz? The prophet is not thinking of any baby to be born in the distant future. He is thinking of a baby to be born within a year. He does not have in his mind any miraculous conception, or any Virgin Birth. Such ideas were utterly foreign to his mind. What he says is that a virgin, or damsel, or maiden, or marriageable young woman, when she brings forth her first baby, will call his name, "God with us," because the danger will have passed away, and the nation will be safe. Isaiah is not interested in the mother, nor is he interested in the baby, he is interested solely in the fact that the baby is going to have a name which will express the joy of the mother over the deliverance of her nation. What he says is nothing more than this: A girl who is now ready to be married, and who may probably be married this week, when she has her first baby, will be able to give it a name which expresses the joy of the nation over its deliverance from these two belligerent kings. Therefore, we must give up the idea that this verse is Messianic, or that it contains any reference whatever to a Virgin Birth or to Jesus of Nazareth.

It was Matthew who caused all the trouble. In the first chapter of his Gospel, he reports the angel of the Lord, saying, "She shall bring forth a son; and thou shalt call his name Jesus; for it is he that shall save his people from their sins." Matthew goes on to say, "All this is come to pass, that it might be fulfilled which was spoken by the Lord through the prophet, saying: 'Behold, the virgin shall be with child, and shall bring forth a son, and they shall call his name Immanuel, which is, being interpreted, 'God with us.' '" This sentence of St. Matthew was long considered final. It convinced multitudes that the prophet was speaking of Jesus and foretelling the Virgin Birth. But a closer study of Matthew's manner of dealing with the Scriptures, frees us from that idea. Matthew was a Jewish Christian. He had been brought up a Jew and loved the Old Testament Scriptures. Later on he had become a follower of Jesus, and being convinced that Jesus was the expected ideal king, he took delight in looking up Old Testament sentences which could in any way be made to bear witness to his Lord. Every expression that might possibly be an allusion to Jesus was seized upon by Matthew and treasured. His way of using the Scriptures is seen in the second chapter of his Gospel. In telling how Herod had sought to seek the young child Jesus to destroy him, and how Joseph had taken Jesus and his mother by night and departed into Egypt, where they remained until the death of Herod, Matthew goes on to say, "That it might be fulfilled which was spoken by the Lord through the prophet saying, 'Out of Egypt did I call my son.' " He is quoting the first words of the 11th chapter of Hosea. Now Hosea in that verse was not referring to the Messiah at all. He was speaking of the Hebrew people. The Hebrew people were God's son. After remaining slaves for hundreds of years in Egypt, God had brought them out of Egypt and led them into the promised land. It is God who is speaking in the 11th chapter of Hosea, "Out of Egypt did I call my son." St. Matthew finds in the experience of Jesus another illustration of how God acts. He does not say that Hosea is thinking of Jesus. All he says is that the words written centuries before, are capable of holding new and larger meanings, and that the experience of the olden times has been repeated on a higher level and with new significance. Just as God, centuries ago brought his son the Hebrew people out of Egypt, so now again he is bringing Jesus his son from Egypt into Galilee.

He then proceeds to tell how Herod slew all the male children that were in Bethlehem, and in all the borders thereof from two years old and under, and then goes on to say, "Then was fulfilled that which was spoken through Jeremiah the prophet, saying, 'A voice was heard in Ramah, weeping and great mourning, Rachel weeping for her children, and she would not be comforted, because they are not.'" Matthew here quotes from the 31st chapter of Jeremiah. When Jeremiah wrote that sentence, he was not thinking of the Messiah. He was not predicting something which was going to take place centuries after his death. He was thinking of the long train of Jewish exiles passing northward on their way to Assyria, and stopping long enough in Ramah, a village five miles north of Jerusalem, in order that the weak and the aged might be sifted out and killed before the caravan proceeded on its melancholy way. With fine poetic power he symbolizes the nation under the figure of Rachel. He pictures the mother of the two great tribes of Joseph and Benjamin looking out from her tomb and bewailing the awful fate of her descendants. Here is no reference whatever to Herod, or to anything that took place in Herod's day, but St. Matthew, when he thinks of the mothers who wept over the death of their babies because of the cruelty of Herod, is reminded of the words of Jeremiah, and he links the two experiences together. Just as mothers centuries before had poured out lamentations over the death of their children, so did mothers in the days of King Herod weep over the death of their children. The experiences of the past were repeated in the present. This is the way in which Matthew made use of Old Testament sentences. He filled them with a richer meaning. And so when Jesus was born in Bethlehem, and his name was called "Jesus," on the ground that he was to save his people from their sins, the evangelist thinks at once of the words of Isaiah. Just as 700 years before a baby had been born which had received a name symbolizing the joy of his mother in the fact that the people were saved, so now another Jewish maiden is rejoicing because she has given birth to a boy who is going to save his people from their sins. Let us then cease to think of the 14th verse of the 7th chapter of Isaiah as containing any reference to the Virgin Mary and her son Jesus.

It is in the first seven verses of chapter 9 that we come upon the first portrait of the ideal king. In order to understand the opening of the paragraph, we must bear in mind that it was the Northern part of Palestine that suffered first and most awfully at the hand of the Assyrian invaders. The Northern tribes were the nearest to Nineveh and most easily gotten at. The Northern tribes were Zebulun and Naphtali, and Tiglath-pileser had trampled them into the mire. Sargon came later and trampled upon them still more cruelly. All the people roundabout Galilee had suffered again and again the horrors of war, and there was lamentation in every home. The prophet believes that such darkness cannot continue forever. The people who have lived in great darkness will some day see a great light. He does not give any date. He says the light is going to shine in the latter time, or, as we would put it, "Sometime." Sometime a great light will shine, and sometime the people around Galilee will rejoice with a great joy. They will rejoice because the tyrant who has afflicted them will be dethroned and all the paraphernalia of war will be burnt up, and there will come a new king upon whose shoulder the government will rest, and his name will be called "Wonderful Counsellor—Mighty God—Everlasting Father—Prince of Peace."

Let us pause for a moment to take in that majestic

title. The words demand explanation, for it is easy for us Occidentals to mistake their meaning. We must remember that it was the custom in the East for nations to give their kings long and high-sounding titles. Rameses II., for instance, had a title which filled six lines. The greater the king, the more titles he had. The Orientals applied to their kings titles which modern nations would shrink from using. For instance, one of the titles of this coming king is to be "Mighty God." We are not to infer from this that he was to be a divine being. Even the Jews had a way of using the word "God," which we could not possibly adopt. In the 10th chapter of St. John's Gospel, Jesus is answering some Jews who are condemning him because he has called himself "The Son of God." He quotes to them the 6th verse of the 82d Psalm, "I said, ye are gods." In that verse the rulers of Palestine are called "gods." They are God's representatives, and therefore there is a sense in which they can carry God's name. They were unrighteous rulers, but nevertheless they were called "gods." The argument of Jesus is, if ordinary rulers are called "gods" in your own Scriptures, then why should you condemn me because I call myself "The Son of God?"

In the 31st chapter of Ezekiel, Nebuchadnezzar is called "God," the same Hebrew word being used which we find in the present title. And therefore the English equivalent of "Mighty God" would be "Mighty Hero," or "Divine Hero," or "Godlike

Hero," a hero in which there is embodied the Divine Energy. "Everlasting Father" must not be made to mean too much. That was an expression often made use of by Assyrians and Babylonians and Egyptians. They called their kings, "Father of Infinity," "Father of Eternity," "Father of Life in Perpetuity," "Father Forever," and when the prophet says that the coming king is going to be called "Mighty God," and "Everlasting Father," he is simply saying that the highest titles ever worn by Assyrian or Egyptian kings will be given to him. His majesty will be unparalleled. He will have four names—"Wonderful Counsellor," "Mighty Hero," "Everlasting Father," "Prince of Peace." He will have every title that the greatest of kings ever had and he will have a new name, the name which no Assyrian or Egyptian King had ever borne—"Prince of Peace." Here, then, is the portrait of the coming king. First of all he has sagacity. He does the thing that is wise. Second, he is mighty. He abounds in strength. Third, he is the guardian or protector of his people. He saves them from harm. Finally he is gentle. He does not rely on violence. He is the Prince of Peace. When one bears in mind the kind of king Ahaz was—foolish, weak, unable to protect, relying always on fortifications and the weapons of war, one can understand how the prophet in dreaming of the ideal king, should give to him as his crowning traits, sagacity and strength and fatherly solicitude and love of peace.

In the first five verses of chapter 11, we have another portrait which is somewhat different. Now, for the first time we are told that the ideal king will come out of the stock of Jesse. Jesse was the father of David. The house has fallen, but nevertheless it has not been extinguished. "There shall come forth a shoot out of the stock of Jesse and a branch out of his roots shall bear fruit." The prophet goes on to tell what kind of king he will be. "The spirit of Jehovah shall rest upon him, the spirit of wisdom and understanding, the spirit of counsel and might, the spirit of knowledge and of the fear of Jehovah." You will observe that the first trait in this portrait is wisdom, and that the second trait is might. In the third trait we find something deeper and more spiritual than any trait which we have found in the first portrait. The king will have the spirit of knowledge and the fear of Jehovah; that is, he will be a pious man, and his delight shall be in the fear of Jehovah. In the first portrait, we had the face of a mighty king and conqueror. Now we find ourself looking into the face of an ideal judge. "He shall not judge after the sight of his eyes, neither decide after the hearing of his ears; but with righteousness shall he judge the poor, and decide with equity for the meek of the earth." The ideal king will be especially solicitous for the rights of the weak and the helpless. He will see that justice is done to all. "Righteousness shall be the girdle of his waist, and faithfulness the girdle of his loins."

This portrait marks an advance over the portrait of chapter 9.

Let us turn now to chapter 32. This paragraph is disappointing. "Behold, a king shall reign in righteousness." That is all that is said of him. The prophet goes on to say that Princes shall rule in justice, and then he seems to turn his back upon all men of rank and to give us a portrait of human nature at its best. It is human personality which is to be the fountain of blessing. It is a man, a noble man who is to give the world what the world most needs. "A man shall be as a hiding place from the wind, and a covert from the tempest, as streams of water in a dry place, as the shade of a great rock in a weary land." You will observe that a note of tenderness is creeping into the prophet's conception of the ideal king. Humanity is exposed to pitiless storms. What humanity needs is shelter. A man after God's ideal will give shelter. The human race is thirsty. It is making a pilgrimage through a desert. Its mouth is parched with thirst, but a man after God's own heart will be like a stream of water in a dry place. Humanity is weary. It is on a long journey. The sun beats down upon it with scorching heat, but a man shall be like the shade of a great rock in a weary land. We Christians have always loved to think that this sketch of the ideal man was fulfilled in Jesus. He has been to multitudes a shelter from the wind, and a covert from the tempest. He has been like a river in a desert, and a shade of a great rock in a weary land. He is the Rock of Ages.

> "Rock of Ages, cleft for me,
> Let me hide myself in Thee."

You will not fail to notice how indefinite and vague the portraits of the ideal king are. We are always in danger of giving the prophets a vision which they did not possess. We look back to Jesus and he stands before us as a distinct and clear-cut figure. He is distinct to us because of what artists have done with their brushes, and because of what the evangelists did with their pens. We imagine because he stands out so clearly before us that he must have stood out clearly before the prophets. We must remember that the prophets looked into a mist. They saw only in part, and they prophesied only in part. We often give them credit for knowing a thousand things they never knew, and for seeing things which their eyes never beheld. Life to them as to us was a great mystery, with only now and then a ray of light breaking through. We spoil the Bible when we make it too supernatural, too miraculous, too magical. The prophets never located the ideal king. They never knew when he was to appear. They never saw distinctly what he was to be. There is no portrait of Jesus in the Old Testament which the most learned Jews of the first century were able to recognize in the prophet of Nazareth. When Jesus appeared, the High Priests did not know him, nor did the elders, nor did the scribes. They knew the Old Testament by heart. They were familiar with every page of it. They were acquainted with all its jots and tittles, but when Jesus appeared they did not believe that he fulfilled the things that had been written. "He was in the world, and the world was made by him, but the world knew him not. He came unto his own, and his own received him not." He claimed to be the Messiah, the ideal king. He did not look like a king. He did not dress like one. He did not act like one, or talk like one. He wore no crown, no royal robe. He had no scepter, no army, no retinue. The Jews at first wanted to make him a king, but he refused to be a king after their conception of kinghood, and so they turned against him and denounced him as an impostor. They dragged him before Pontius Pilate. The Roman Procurator looked at him and said, "Are you a king?" And Jesus replied, "I am." Later on he was turned over to the Roman soldiers who dressed him up in order to make him look like a king. One of them put on him an old scarlet cloak. Another put in his hand a reed which looked like a scepter. Another went out and broke off some twigs of a thorny bush and twisted them into a circlet which he jammed down on Jesus' head. That was his crown. They set him on a bench which was his throne. They then came before him, kneeling in mock reverence, each one saying, "Hail King! Hail

King!" They soon grew weary of that, and blind-folded his eyes. When he could not see, they went up one after the other and slapped him on the face, saying, "Tell us who was it that hit you." After they grew weary of that, they spat on him, in order to show their contempt for a king of his style. Finally, one jerked the reed out of his hand and struck him over the head with it. Roman soldiers despised a king like Jesus. When the prisoner was brought back to the Procurator, the Procurator asked, "What shall I do with your king?" They cried out, "Crucify him," and so Pilate ordered him to be crucified. He wrote an inscription which was to be nailed to the cross above his head, "This is Jesus of Nazareth, the King of the Jews." When the Chief Priests saw the inscription, they were in-furiated. They rushed to Pilate, saying in rage, "Do not write that, write, 'He said, I am King of the Jews.'" But Pilate brushed them aside with the petulant remark, "What I have written, I have written."

"Who do men say I am?" Jesus asked his disciples one day when they had gone off into a secluded place by themselves. Peter replied, "They say you are one of the prophets." "Who do you say that I am?" And to this Peter replied, "I think you are the Messiah," to which Jesus replied, "You are right, Simon, and I am going to build my church on men who believe that!"

IX

A WARLESS WORLD

If one were asked to write down the six most often repeated sentences in the first thirty-nine chapters of the Book of Isaiah, he would include this sentence in his list: "They shall beat their swords into plowshares, and their spears into pruning hooks; nation shall not lift up sword against nation, neither shall they learn war any more." If one were asked to write the three most famous sentences of Isaiah, the Son of Amoz, I suspect that this sentence would have to be one of the three. There are some who think it is the greatest sentence which Isaiah ever wrote.

The sentence suggests an interesting literary problem. If you will read the first paragraph in the second chapter of Isaiah, and then read the first paragraph in the fourth chapter of Micah, you will find that the two paragraphs are the same. They are not simply similar to each other, they are identical. They express the same ideas in the same sequence and in the same language. God never inspires two men to say the same thing in the same way. We, therefore, know that Isaiah is quoting

April 5, 1925.

[160]

Micah or that Micah is quoting Isaiah, or that both
prophets are quoting an earlier writer, or that some
later editor has inserted in both books a quotation
from some anonymous prophet who flourished at a
later date. There are arguments for each one of
these four positions, but we have no time to go into
that just now. All I can do is to give you my own
conclusion. I am convinced that Isaiah is the author
of this sentence. My reasons are four in number.
In the first place, Isaiah was one of the greatest
spiritual geniuses of all time. He was the man who
painted the first portrait of the Messiah, and it was
he who developed the doctrine of the Remnant. He
pointed out the place and power of the minority in
the development of the human race. This idea of
a warless world, then, is not beyond him. It is the
kind of idea which one might expect to spring from
his wonderful brain.

In the second place, he was a master of language.
He wrote in a great style. Anyone who is sensitive
to the music and splendor of speech, falls in love
with this sentence about the swords and plowshares.
Only a great artist can use words after that fashion.
The sentence sounds like Isaiah.

We know that Isaiah was a hater of war. When
in the 9th chapter he sets out to tell us about the
ideal king, he begins by burning up all the paraphernalia of battle in a great bonfire. He then proceeds
to tell us the name of the coming king. He will have
many titles, but his highest title will be "Prince of

Peace." The man who painted the portrait of the "Prince of Peace" might be expected to give us a vision of a warless world.

In the fourth place Isaiah was an internationalist. Above all the prophets of Israel he had the international mind. His horizon was wide. He moved easily in the great spaces of international thought and action. For all these four reasons I am convinced that Isaiah is the author of this sentence. Micah was a younger contemporary of Isaiah, and it is easier for a younger man to quote an older man than for an older man to quote a younger man. There is no record of any preceding prophet to whom we could with any certainty trace this sentence, and there is no conclusive proof that it came from a prophet of a later date. Let us assume, then, that it was Isaiah who gave to mankind the prophecy of a warless world.

Let us look at the sentence. Let us lay our mind on it in order that we may feel what a wonderful sentence it is. It is wonderful because of its age. It is 2600 years old. It was born in the 8th century B.C. That was the age of Tiglath-pileser, the Alexander the Great, the Genghis Khan, the Tamerlane, and the Napoleon I. of that century. In that century war was the pastime of kings and the glory of them. It was by war that a king won imperishable renown. It was natural to fight, and normal to engage in battle. Assyria was a military power, and so also was Egypt. All the kingdoms around

Judah believed in war and practiced it. Where did Isaiah get his idea of a warless world? Certainly not from Tiglath-pileser or from Shalmaneser or from Sargon or from Sennacherib. Surely not from any Egyptian king. It is certain that he did not get it from any king of Moab or Edom or Philistia or Phoenicia. He did not get it from any King of Judah. Uzziah was a great warrior. He took delight in the instruments and victories of war. He was proud of his army and navy. Isaiah did not get his idea from Ahaz, for Ahaz was an enthusiastic believer in preparedness and relied on his fortifications and military equipment. Where did Isaiah get his idea of a warless world? How surprising that in the 8th century there should live a man who could see that there is no place in the ideal world for war—that war is only a transient horror that will some time pass away—that war is not after the mind of God and will some day be banished from the world. Where did Isaiah get that idea? I think the most rational explanation is that the idea came to him from God. Here we have an instance of what is known as inspiration. The doctrine of inspiration has often been presented in such crude and irrational ways, that some people have given it up altogether. They do not believe that any men have ever been inspired. But why should we discard the idea of inspiration? Why should it be deemed incredible that an idea should slip from the mind of God into the mind of man? Why should we find it hard to believe that the Spirit of the Eternal can so light up a man's mind as to enable him to see things which other men cannot see? Peter put it right when he said that holy men of old spake as they were moved by the Holy Spirit. Isaiah wrote this sentence about a warless world because he was moved by the Spirit of Almighty God.

That the idea came from God is evidenced by the fact that it cannot be destroyed. It is an idea that will not die. The human mind is wonderfully prolific and it gives birth to an infinite number of ideas and conceptions and notions and hopes and fancies and dreams, and most of these after a little while grow weak and die. Only a small fraction of the ideas born in the mind survive. Here is an idea which survives. It is 2600 years old and yet it still lives and is more alive today than it has ever been since it came out of Isaiah's brain. Think of the enemies it has had to meet. Think of the floods it has come through without being drowned. Think of the fires it has passed through without being burned. Think of the swords which have hacked at it without cutting it to pieces. Think of the spears that have been driven through it without putting an end to its life. Think of the mighty warrior kings who have trampled on it, and think of the military experts in gold braid who have poured out upon it the acid of their biting contempt, and yet it still lives. It is alive in the minds of more people today than at any other time in the 2600 years.

This is all the more surprising when we remember that the hope has never been fulfilled. The dream has never been realized. Through 2600 years there has been continuous disappointment. Every generation has looked forward to a warless world, and every generation has looked forward in vain. In each succeeding century through twenty-six centuries, bold-hearted men have dared to proclaim the speedy advent of a warless world. They have all phophesied in vain, but in spite of the disappointment the world goes right on dreaming of a time when war shall be no more. Our generation is thinking of such a time, although our generation is the most disappointed of all generations that have ever been. We were told that the age of war was ended—that never again would there be a great war. Long conclusive arguments were framed to prove to us that a world war was impossible, or that if such a war ever came it would last at the longest only a few weeks. And then after all these beautiful predictions the world war came and lasted, not a few weeks but four years, and the human heart was filled with a disappointment that was an anguish. But nevertheless we are still looking forward to a warless world. We cannot give up that hope. We cannot cease to dream. The idea of a warless world is here, and we cannot get rid of it. It is impossible to shake it off. We cannot run away from it. It pursues us. It haunts us, and there is no escape. It goes before us. It is a gleam which keeps flashing in our eyes, and we are following it. We cannot do anything else. This would indicate that the idea is rooted in the mind of God.

The persistency of this idea is mightily impressive. The universe is at times freakish. Now and then she does things for a little while, and then ceases to do them. There are phenomena that appear only for a season and then vanish forever. Science is not greatly interested in the things which appear only to disappear. She gives her attention to the things that persist. When she finds a phenomenon continuing through centuries and ages, she becomes respectful in its presence and studies it with great care. She knows that that phenomenon has a vast significance. She does her utmost to find out what it means. Here in the life of humanity we have a phenomenon which persists. A man 2600 years ago got the idea that war would some day be banished, and that idea has persisted down to the present hour. It seems to be as indestructible as the world itself, and we do well to study it with awe. If the idea cannot be destroyed it would seem that this is the Lord's doing, and it must be wonderful in our eyes.

It is to be noted that Isaiah did not set the time when his dream would come true. He begins by saying, "In the latter days." That is exceedingly indefinite. It is a phrase which he likes. He meant by that something similar to what we mean by "sometime." He does not say that there is to be a warless world in this generation, or in the next.

He contents himself by saying that sometime war will be no more. A mediocre man always sets the day. He takes delight in telling you the exact time when a certain thing is to take place. That is an unfailing sign of mediocrity. Only men who are blear-eyed ever deal in dates. When you hear a man predict with confidence the occurrence of some long wished for event on a date which he names, do not listen to him. When you hear men proclaiming with great gusto that a certain thing is going to happen in the lifetime of men now living, put them down as blind leaders. Every one who believes them will find himself at last in a ditch. The great seers of humanity do not set dates. They see too far into the structure of the universe and into the nature of the human mind to fix events in the calendar. They understand that it is not for them to know the times or the seasons which God has placed in his own power. They are satisfied to know that there is a Holy Spirit in this world, and that when he comes upon a man, that man has strength to do the work appointed him. Isaiah was not troubled about dates. "Sometime," he said, "swords will be beaten into plowshares, and nations will learn war no more." That is enough for us to know. If we can only be certain that some time war will be abolished, we can go on working with enthusiasm and unfailing vigor. We can work year after year without disappointment or despair, and when at last the time comes for us to die we can pass on the torch to the hands of others who will carry it down the future. Even though the swords have not yet been beaten into plowshares, we can pass from this world into the next absolutely certain that our labor has not been in vain in the Lord.

When I have spoken of this hope of Isaiah as a dream, I have not meant by that an idle fancy. "Dream" is a word often used in a derogatory sense. We talk of "Day Dreams," which are so many foolish imaginings. We use the word "Dream" in the sense of a bubble of the imagination—a phantom of the brain—a chimera—an illusion, insubstantial and of no account. I am not using the word "Dream" in any such sense. By "Dream" I mean a vision of reality, a vision that is solid and that rests on Eternal foundations. Isaiah is not giving utterance to a pretty notion. He is stating something that is going to be, and he says clearly how it is going to come to pass. Many of us have never paid attention to the words immediately preceding the sentence about which we now are thinking. This particular sentence is so beautiful we have not cared to study anything which comes before it or which follows it. We are like little children caught by things that glitter, and if a sentence on the page of Scripture only glitters in our eyes, we stop and say, "How pretty," and "how nice," and "how lovely," "I think I will memorize that." We call it a "gem," and we use it as we would use any other gem. We wear it on our finger like a ruby or a diamond. We do not make it a principle by which we live. But as a practical man, Isaiah was interested in the method by which the warless world was to come. It is not enough to think about a warless world, or to wish for such a world, or to talk about it. A warless world is an achievement—something to be achieved by man. It is not something to be handed to us by the Almighty, but something which we ourselves must win. It is not to come down upon us like a beautiful exhalation from the skies. It is a solid reality to be built up from the earth on which we live. Isaiah understands all this, and so before he speaks about the swords being beaten into plowshares, he tells us just how that glorious time is going to come. We have been thinking simply of the last twenty-seven words of a paragraph, and have paid no attention to the hundred and ten words which precede these. Let me read them to you: "And it shall come to pass in the latter days, that the mountain of the Lord's house shall be established on the top of the mountains, and shall be exalted above the hills; and all nations shall flow unto it. And many peoples shall go and say, Come ye, and let us go up to the mountain of the Lord, to the house of the God of Jacob; and he will teach us of his ways, and we will walk in his paths; for out of Zion shall go forth the law, and the word of the Lord from Jerusalem. And he will judge between the nations, and will decide concerning many peoples." All that must happen before nations shall beat their swords into plowshares and learn war no more.

Let me now translate the words which I have read. The Hebrew words have been translated into English words, but they have not yet been translated into American thought. It is not until ideas are translated into American thought that they have any influence over us. This is what Isaiah says: "Sometime my nation is going to lead the world." You will remember that he is painting an ideal picture. That is the way he is sure things ought to be. His own nation ought to lead the world. That is what we Americans think when we are thinking at our best. America ought to lead the world. That is our ideal in English. Isaiah says that his capital is going to be lifted up above all the other capitals of the world. In his own poetic way, he says it is going to be on a mountain. That is an orator's way of saying that the capital of his country is going to be above other capitals in its ideals and practices. Because it is so high above them, other nations will flow unto it. Mark that surprising expression—he has placed his country on the top of a mountain, and now he says, other nations will flow up to it. Can nations flow uphill? They can. In the physical universe we expect things to flow down, but in the spiritual universe they often flow up. There is not only a law of gravitation, but there is also a law of attraction. According to the law of gravitation things flow down, but according to the law of attraction things sometimes flow up. Hold your magnet a little distance above the table, and if there are iron filings on the table, those iron filings will flow up. Even iron can flow up. Let one nation be exalted above other nations in moral traits and spiritual vision, and other nations will be attracted. They will be lifted up by the nation which is above them. Jesus gave expression to that great law when he said: "And I, if I be lifted up, will draw all men unto me." He knew that when he died upon the cross, men everywhere would see that he was above Pontius Pilate and Caiaphas, and all the rest of them. It has all come out even as he said. We are not drawn to Pontius Pilate or to Caiaphas, or to any of the Chief Priests and Elders, we are drawn to Jesus, and the reason we are so drawn is because he is so high above us. It is the ideal which causes us to flow up. Nations are going to say to one another: "Let us go up to the house of the God of Jacob. He will teach us his ways, and we will walk in his paths. He will teach us the principles of life, and we will practice them, and God himself will be judge among the nations. The Almighty will be the arbiter. Disputes will be referred to him. He is the Eternal Reason, and men will come to put their confidence in reason. They will not rely on brute force. They will acknowledge the supremacy of conscience. They will bow before Righteousness, and when they do that, there will be no further use for the instruments of destruction. Men will then beat their swords into plowshares and their spears into pruning hooks. When all international differences are referred to the arbitrament of reason, then nation shall not lift up sword against nation, neither shall they learn war any more."

Here, then, we have given to us the method by which we are to achieve a warless world. A warless world is coming through religion. A man saw that 2600 years ago. He saw it because his eyes were touched by the Spirit of the Eternal. There are men of reputed intelligence in our day who do not see that yet. It is amazing how naïve and simpleminded we mortals can be. There are many who have told us that a warless world will come through science. Before the World War came, these prophets were everywhere vocal and exuberant. They were sure that science would put an end to war, but by the Great War we were taught that science only gives us a sharper sword and a longer spear. That is all it will ever do. It was science that made the Great War horrible. It was because of the abundance of our science that we shed so much blood. It was because we were so scientific that we dug so many graves. There is no salvation for humanity through science. Others have always claimed that a warless world would come through education. It is because people are ignorant that nations fight, so it has been said. Only build more universities and schools, give the people of the world access to books,

and then the swords will disappear. If by education
you mean a knowledge of the sciences and philoso-
phies and languages, you are talking sheer nonsense.
There is nothing in education to give us a warless
world. We never had so much education as we had
in the year 1913. We had what we called the
"Higher Learning," and we were proud of it, and
nowhere was learning so high as it was in Germany,
and it was in Germany that humanity started on its
journey to hell. There is no salvation in education,
unless by education you mean the development of the
human mind and heart in the School of Jesus Christ.
There were bold prophets who said a warless world
would come through commerce. Commerce is a
great wizard, and has a magical fashion of linking
continents together and interlacing the interests of
separated peoples, and the argument was plausible
and it seemed convincing that under the beneficent
influence of commere, war would pass away. But
in the Great War we had an example of what commerce is able to do. If commerce is a great peace-
maker, commerce can also be a great war-maker.
Her insatiable greed for new markets and raw
materials and cheap labor, is one of the greatest in-
centives to war. When the Great War came, we
saw that commerce was one of the devils who pushed
us into the fire. There is no hope for this world
through commerce. There were many who claimed
that we could get a warless world only through in-
dustrial organization. Men assured us that when

the wage-earners formed themselves into great organizations, and these organizations were bound to similar organizations in other lands, then the nations would learn war no more. But when the curtain went up and the tragedy began, we saw that wage-earners were fighting their brothers on every one of the fields of blood. A warless world will never come through labor unions or organized socialism.

Others were certain that war would end war. When we found ourselves in the midst of the Great War, many superficial people endeavored to comfort themselves by assuring us that that war would end war. The Great War gave us an opportunity to find out how much sense there is in that expectation. Here was the mightiest war of all time, a giant among giants, a very Goliath in the military camp—a superwar, and if war can ever be pounded into pulp by war, then the world has had a chance to see that feat accomplished. But the Great War did not kill war, for otherwise, why is it that the nations are all preparing for another war? Today we have peace, but it is the peace of exhaustion. Nations are not fighting because they are too weak. The spirit is willing, but the flesh is weak. Humanity is in a hospital where she must stay for a season until she recuperates from her bruises and wounds, and then she will fight again. There is no hope for a warless world through war. War only intensifies all the hatreds and kindles all the passions to a hotter flame.

Nor is there any hope for a warless world through the fear of war. All this talk about obtaining security through preparedness is on a level with the frenzied ravings of lunatics. We never can achieve a warless world through the piling up of the instruments of slaughter. How then can we get it? Only in one way. Only through religion. Only when men come to God and allow him to instruct them in his ways will it be possible for war to be abolished. Only when nations are ready to submit all their disputes to reason will the swords be beaten into plowshares and spears into pruning hooks. A man saw that 2600 years ago. Many men reputed learned cannot see it yet.

A warless world is coming through the church; that is, through organized believers in the Eternal Reason. There is an expression in this paragraph which may have escaped your notice, "Out of Zion shall go forth the law." Zion was a mountain, or, as we would say, a hill, on which the temple was built. "Out of Zion" therefore means, "Out of the temple." The temple was the symbol of the church. What Isaiah says is, "Out of the church shall go forth the law." The word "Law" is not the best translation for the Hebrew. You will observe that in the margin the revisers have put the word, "Instruction." That is the word which you ought to introduce into the text. Out of the church shall go forth the instruction which will enable the nations to beat their swords into plowshares. This is the supreme work of the church. The Jewish Church would not accept its responsibility. It would not accept the Ideal King, and so God passed by the Jewish Church and gave authority to the Christian Church, the body of believers who have accepted Jesus as the Ideal King. It is for the Christian Church to teach the nations the principles of God, and to persuade them to walk in his ways. It is for the church to give instruction to the diplomats and the journalists, and the literati all over the world, for without this Christian instruction there is no hope for mankind. What a privilege it is to belong to the Church of Christ, and what an honor, and what a responsibility it brings. O members of the Church of Christ, I salute you as soldiers of the Army of the Prince of Peace! You are followers of a leader who says, "Put up your sword, for all they that take the sword shall perish with the sword." You have enlisted in a great campaign which is not to end until war has been banished from our world. When men and women unite with the Tabernacle, the first thing they are asked to do, is to partake of the Communion. In this they swear allegiance to their Commander, the Prince of Peace. The bread and wine are memorials of a man who gave himself a ransom for many, who surrendered his life at the hands of force, that reason might rule the world.

X

THE DAY OF THE LORD

If anyone should ask why in my list of seven cardinal ideas of Isaiah, I do not include the idea of Immortality—an idea peculiarly appropriate for a sermon on Easter Sunday—my reply is that the idea of Immortality was not an idea in which Isaiah had any interest. It was scarcely in all his thought. He was not enthusiastic about life beyond death. The fate of the soul after death did not concern him. For his mind, the other world had no attraction. This is surprising. Isaiah, the son of Amoz, was one of the greatest of all the Hebrew prophets. Some scholars would say he was the greatest spiritual genius of all time. He was one of the most eloquent preachers who have ever spoken for God. He preached in the City of Jerusalem for forty years, and possibly longer, and yet in all that time he never, so far as we know, delivered a message on life after death. We are almost certain he never touched on that subject for the reason that we have an account of his dealing with his friend Hezekiah at a critical juncture in the latter's life. Hezekiah was the King of Judah, and the king and the

April 12, 1925.

prophet were intimate friends. One day Hezekiah fell ill, and his illness was of such a character as to lead Isaiah to feel it was an illness unto death. Looking at him as he lay upon his bed, Isaiah frankly told him the time had arrived for him to set his house in order, for he was going to die. Not one word of consolation did the prophet speak to him. Not one ray of cheer or of hope did he cast upon the future. All that Isaiah could do was to announce that the time had arrived when the king must die. On hearing the fateful words, the king did what any other man would have done, he turned his face to the wall and began to pray. To every man there comes soon or late, an hour in which the only thing he can do is to talk to God. Hezekiah prayed, and as he prayed he wept. He did not want to die. Death is a great intruder. It upsets our plans, it tramples on our dreams. The king felt his work was not completed. He had many things yet to do for Jerusalem. Moreover he had no son to whom he could leave his crown. He begged God to let him live, and God granted his request. He allowed the king to live fifteen years longer. In his days of rejoicing, Hezekiah wrote a poem in which he expressed his gratitude to God for the mercy shown him. That poem is recorded in the 38th chapter of Isaiah. The surprising feature of the poem to us is its omission of any joyful reference to the future life. He is happy because he is to live a few years more in this world, but he has

[178]

no joyful hope of living forever. Here are a few of his doleful references to life after death: "Sheol cannot praise Thee." "Death cannot celebrate Thee." "They that go down into the pit cannot hope for Thy truth." "The living, the living, he shall praise Thee, as I do this day."

Here, then, we have a Hebrew King of the 8th century before Christ, who has no doctrine of Immortality which makes his heart glad. He was no ordinary king. He was religious, a great moral reformer. He left a mark on the life of his nation which endured through generations. A Hebrew historian writing in the Second Book of Kings, declares that among all the kings who came after Hezekiah, not one was his equal, nor was there his equal among his predecessors. This devout Hebrew King found no solace in the thought of continued life after death. He and Isaiah were alike in limiting their thought to the life which now is.

We are not to infer from this that these men did not believe in the continued existence of the soul beyond the tomb. They believed that men existed after death, but their existence was ghostly and shadowy, a pallid shade of the life which men live upon the earth. They believed in a world of the dead, which world they called "Sheol." It was a huge cavern located under the earth, very dark and gloomy, and men shuddered at the thought of descending into it. This idea of the future world comes out again and again in the Old Testament

Scriptures. In the seventh chapter of the Book of Job, we read, "He that goeth down to Sheol shall come up no more," and in the 14th chapter we read, "Till the heavens be no more, they shall not awake, nor be roused out of their sleep." The colors are still darker in the Book of Ecclesiastes, where, we are told, "The dead know not anything." One of the greatest of the Hebrew prophets and one of the most religious of the Hebrew Kings are dumb on the subject of Immortality. This is an interesting fact to ponder on Easter Sunday, for it confirms what Paul wrote to Timothy, that Jesus had brought life and immortality to light. The idea of continued existence was in men's minds, but it lay in the shadow until Jesus Christ brought it out into the day. It lay for centuries at the back of men's minds, furnishing neither joy nor strength, until Jesus Christ brought it to the front of the mind and made it a hope and a joy. Not till Jesus Christ lived and died and rose again, did men ever sing of life after death.

The prophets of Israel looked forward, but they did not look beyond death. Their vision was limited by the world which now is. But they always looked forward. They saw in the future what they called the "Day of the Lord." That Day of the Lord would arrive for men in this world. But in that idea of the Day of the Lord, there lay the germ which in the course of centuries was to be developed into the Christian doctrine of Immortality.

THE DAY OF THE LORD

Let me trace for you this morning the development of this idea of the Day of the Lord.

The idea was in the world long before Isaiah's day. It first meets us in the Book of Amos, but it was Isaiah who first gave it prominence in the history of religious thought. Isaiah was driven to think of the Day of the Lord by his conception of Deity. To him God is the Infinite Righteousness, the Infinite Reason, and the Infinite Holiness. He is King of the whole earth. Being righteous and rational and holy, he must desire a world full of justice and reason and purity. Alas, the world is not this. The world is full of corruption and injustice and misery. Virtue often walks in rags, and vice often rides in satin. The world is filled with injustices and inequalities and moral confusion. As Lowell puts it—"Right forever on the scaffold, wrong forever on the throne." There is an ideal world, and there is also an actual world, and these two worlds hang side by side before the eyes of every thoughtful man. The two worlds clash. They contradict each other. How can they be reconciled? There is only one of two things which we can do. We can deny that God is a moral Being who recognizes moral distinctions and moral values. We can say that he is not interested in the behavior of men, and that it matters nothing to him what men think or say or do. Or we can say that He is all wise and all good and Almighty, and that his "day" has not yet arrived. There will come a day in which

[181]

his purposes will become clear, his plan will be made manifest, his ideas will be realized, and his character will be vindicated. At present we are living in the day of man, but sometime there will come the day of the Lord, and in that day all oppositions will be swept away, and the Lord God Almighty will be exalted as the rightful sovereign of every land and of every heart. There will be a day, a glorious day, in which the will of God will be done on earth even as it is done in heaven. The prophets were sure of the coming of this day of the Lord.

There were two ways of painting this day. They sometimes painted it as a day of darkness, and sometimes as a day of light, sometimes as a day of tribulation, and sometimes as a day of great rejoicing. The colors with which they painted it depended upon their standpoint. If they were contemplating the fate of the wicked, the day was dark; if they were thinking of the rewards of the godly, the day was bright. The day of the Lord would mean different things to different classes of persons. Isaiah knew how to paint both styles of picture, and I ask you to look at two of them this morning. The first is the last eleven verses of the second chapter, and the second is the first nine verses of the eleventh chapter. The first is a day of darkness, and second is a day of light.

In the second chapter, the prophet looks out upon a world that because of its prosperity has become haughty and vainglorious. That is always the im-

mediate effect of prosperity, it makes men proud
and bumptious. They feel that they know it all, and
can do it all, and have no need of Divine assistance.
Isaiah looks out upon his generation, full of strut
and brag, and proclaims a day of the Lord on which
all this vanity and boasting will be brought down to
the dust. He begins with the cedars of Lebanon.
Before going on, let me call attention to a habit
of the Hebrew prophets which must be taken into
account when we attempt to interpret their message,
because it is a habit which is peculiar to them and
which is common to them all. To them the material
universe was small and it was also human. The
earth was the center of everything, and the heavens
were an appendage of the earth. The heavens re-
volved around the earth and were created for the
earth, and everything which went on upon the earth
had its effect reflected in the heavens. The Book of
Isaiah opens, as you remember, with an appeal to
the heavens: "Hear, O heavens," cries the prophet,
taking it for granted that the heavens will be interested in the story of Israel's sin. Nature is sympathetic with man and shares man's joys and his
sorrows. If humanity becomes headstrong and
puffed up, then nature will also be brought down in
the downfall of man. Everything that is lifted up
will feel the force of the divine wrath. To the
Jews, the tallest objects which had life in them were
the Cedars of Lebanon. A Jew on looking northward from Palestine saw always the snowy summits

of the mountain range of Lebanon on whose vast sides there stood mighty cedars, some of them thousands of years old. When he looked eastward across the Jordan, his eyes fell on the great oak forests of the Plateau of Bashan. These cedars and oaks were dear to the poets and preachers of Israel, and became to them symbols of religious truths and spiritual ideas. Isaiah looks at them and says, "They are coming down! all of them are coming down! the very mountains are coming down and the hills also in the coming day of the Lord!" Having declared the humiliation of nature, he turns his eyes on civilization. The world of man is also coming down. He seizes first upon its most conspicuous features. The lofty towers and the fortified walls are coming down. Men were vain of their military equipment then as they are now. Nations believed in preparedness and sought security by the creation of instruments of destruction. Isaiah saw the transitoriness and foolishness of all this display of the enginery of force. He was not impressed by the boastfulness and swagger of the military chieftains. The whole war system was coming down, he said, in the day of the Lord. And so also would commerce be humbled. The merchant princes were loftyminded then as many of their successors are today. The prophet seizes upon the ships of Tarshish as symbols of this pomp and pride. Tarshish was a city in Spain, and Spain was the western end of the world. Only the biggest ships could make their way to Tarshish. The world was thrilled by the sight of vessels which could sail to the end of the earth. All this pageantry of commerce, said the prophet, will be brought down. "The loftiness of man shall be brought down, and the haughtiness of men shall be brought low, and God alone shall be exalted in that day." The preacher goes on to predict the end of idolatry. Men have been worshiping the things which their own hands have created, but all of these idols are going to vanish. Men will see their uselessness and impotency and will throw them away. In their disgust they will hurl them to the moles and the bats, creatures which live in the darkness and love it, and men themselves will endeavor to hide themselves in dark places, crawling into the caves of the rocks, in order to escape the terror of God when he arises to shake mightily the earth. What an amazing man this is in the mastery of language, in the painting of word-pictures, in the exposition and glorifying of ideas. When you listen to him you are listening to one of the great orators of all time.

Isaiah was a master in the painting of pictures of tribulation and woe. No one ever surpassed him in mixing the hues of midnight and eclipse, but he was equally gifted in the painting of pictures filled with sunlight and glory. Let us now turn to the first nine verses of chapter 11. Here we have the day of the Lord painted in the colors of the morning. The day of the Lord has inaugurated a golden age. A King is going to rule, upon whom the spirit of the Almighty has descended. In his brain there will be wisdom and understanding, and in his heart there will be piety and spiritual knowledge. He will be a judge, and his judgments will be righteous altogether. He will mete out justice to the poor and to the meek, the classes who have been long neglected, and who because of their weakness have been trampled on by the heels of might. To these neglected and long-suffering people, the ruler of the nation will grant full justice, and wicked men who have for generations sat in high places and lorded it over their fellow men, will not be able to stand in the presence of this Ruler, of whose waist righteousness shall be the girdle, and who shall be faithful in the performance of all the duties which he owes to God and men. Cruelty will vanish and violence will disappear, and in this golden time, even the animal creation will be transformed. At this point, we must pause again to meditate for a moment on another trait of the Hebrew prophets. They looked upon the animal world as a part of the human world. Men and animals are bound up together in a great cosmic scheme, and whatever is done in the human world is reflected in the world of animals. If man goes down, the animals go with him, if man goes up the animals go up also. When cruelty and violence disappear from the homes of men, these will also vanish from the haunts of animals. When men cease to devour one another, animals will also give up their cruel treatment of one another. Animals which have for centuries been mutual foes, will lie down together as comrades and friends. The wolf shall dwell with the lamb, the leopard shall lie down with the kid. Peace and good-will will take the place of hatred and blood-shed. The age-long enmity between wild animals and the human race will entirely pass away, and a little child will lead a young lion, and a baby will play with an asp without suffering harm, and a child who has just been weaned will put his hand unafraid on the most venomous of serpents. There will be no creature anywhere which will hurt or destroy, for the earth shall be full of the knowledge of God as the waters cover the sea. What an imag-ination! What rhetoric! What eloquence! In the presence of this Son of Amoz, you are standing before the Shakespeare among the prophets.

It is because of this bold use of the imagination and this gorgeousness of verbal imagery, that many persons find it difficult or impossible to interpret aright the prophets of Israel. We Occidentals are in our ordinary moods literalists, and a literalist can-not enter the kingdom of the prophetic mind. A literalist makes havoc of the Bible. He makes it ridiculous, incredible, demoralizing. He kills the Scripture. The letter always kills, only the Spirit can make alive. Let us take two passages of Scripture as illustrations of highly imaginative language, one from the Old Testament, the other from the New

Testament. Sometime, probably two hundred and fifty years after Isaiah's day, there lived a prophet by the name of "Joel" who painted an unforgettable picture of the Day of the Lord. In that picture Joel sketched the glorious time when the spirit of God was going to be poured out upon all mankind. Only upon isolated individuals at rare intervals had the Spirit of God been poured out preceding Joel's day, but the prophet, gazing into the future, saw a day when the Spirit of the Eternal would be poured out upon all classes, the slaves as well as the freeborn, the young as well as the old, the women as well as the men. The privilege of speaking for God would belong to everybody. And this wonderful spiritual event would be accompanied by physical phenomena equally wonderful. There would be "wonders in the heavens above, and signs on the earth beneath, blood and fire and vapor of smoke, the sun would be turned into darkness and the moon into blood, before the day of the Lord should come, that great and notable day."

It is fortunate for us that we have an apostolic interpretation of this prophecy of Joel. If Peter was ever on any day of his life inspired, he was certainly inspired on the day of Pentecost. He was on that day so filled with the Spirit of God that he dared to do things he could not have done on any day preceding this, and when he interprets a paragraph of ancient prophecy, we are justified in concluding that his interpretation is correct. When the

Holy Spirit came into the hearts of the one hundred and twenty men and women in the upper room, Peter saw in that experience a fulfillment of Joel's words. The glorious time had at last arrived when all classes and all ages and both sexes could speak for God. He quotes not only the words of the prophet concerning the pouring out of the Spirit, but he goes on to quote what Joel had said about the wonders in the heaven, how the sun was turned into darkness and the moon into blood. But where on the Day of Pentecost were the wonders in the heaven above? Where were the blood and the fire and the vapor of smoke? Was the sun turned into darkness and the moon into blood? What means, then, this description of phenomena that never happened? The prophet is doing what the prophets always did. He is representing the physical creation as responding to what is going on in the lives of men. Nature is not impassive. She is sympathetic. She is not indifferent, she is alive and plays a part. Joel could not conceive of God pouring out his Spirit upon all flesh without that great act being accompanied by a special manifestation of the divine power in the realm of nature. This talk about the wonders in the heaven and the blood and the fire and the smoke is the physical drapery of a spiritual event. It is the poetic embellishment of a spiritual fact. The prophet in this imagery is not talking to the intellect, he is talking to the imagination and the heart. He wants to thrill the imagination and move

[189]

the heart to a joyful appreciation of the vast and eternal significance of a spiritual experience. The blood and fire and smoke are simply the frame of the picture.

In the twenty-first chapter of the last book of the New Testament there is a picture of the City of God. The Book of Revelation is a specimen of Apocalyptic literature, and Apocalyptic is a special form of prophecy. The picture of the New Jerusalem is probably the best known picture to be found in our Bible. The foundations of the city are gems, the streets are of gold and the gates are pearls. This is not a picture of heaven, as many persons have imagined, but a picture of civilization perfected. The City of God is not above the clouds, it is here on this earth. It is not after death, it is before death. The writer has strained language to the utmost in his effort to present a picture of fascinating beauty, but those of us who bring to it a literalistic mind are not attracted by it. We would not care to live in such a city. How uncomfortable it would be! We would far rather live in dear, dingy old New York with its littered streets and its noisy cobblestones, and its worn-out asphalt, and with no gates at all, than in that gorgeous city with its streets of gold. But this picture in the New Testament is not prose, it is poetry. It is not written for the intellect, but for the imagination. The writer has swept together all the precious stones he has ever heard of, and has massed them in a glittering foundation. He has lined the streets with gold because gold is precious, and he has made every gate out of a pearl because pearls are both precious and beautiful. He has put everything outside of the city which is ugly and hateful and vile. He has put inside of the city everything which is radiant and precious and beautiful, and he holds it before our eyes all lit up with the light which falls from God's face. He is not talking prose to the intellect, he is talking poetry to the heart. All he wants to do is to thrill the imagination and move the soul by a picture of indescribable loveliness, a hint of the loveliness we shall see in human society when God's will is done upon earth even as it is done in heaven.

The Day of the Lord! That is a fluid phrase. It flows from one form to another. Sometimes it is "the Day of the Lord," sometimes "a Day of the Lord," sometimes, "that Day," sometimes it is a period rather than a day, it is "that time" or "the last days," or "the latter days," and sometimes it is "the great and terrible day." Its content was fluctuating. Each prophet poured into it the meaning which he wished to carry to his generation. It was a day seen with great distinctness, sometimes with startling vividness. It was usually placed in the early future, and the greater the oppression and misery of the people, the nearer loomed the Day of the Lord. The human heart when sorely stricken found relief in a day of deliverance which was near at hand. It is one thing in Amos, and a richer thing in Isaiah. It is a narrow thing in Habakkuk, a wider thing in Zephaniah. It is a day of judgment on the nation in Jeremiah, and a day of judgment on individuals in Ezekiel. In Joel it is a day of judgment on this earth. In the second Isaiah we meet for the first time the idea of "a new heaven and a new earth." Gradually the day of the Lord began to take in the dead as well as the living. In the vision of an anonymous prophet who lived probably about three hundred years before Christ, the righteous dead rise to share in the glory of the Day of the Lord, and in the last chapter of the Book of Daniel—all the dead arise, both the wicked and the righteous, to receive at the hands of God condemnation or reward. When we open our New Testament we find Paul writing about "The day of our Lord Jesus Christ."

We Christians call the first day of the week, "The Lord's Day," or "The Day of the Lord." That was the name given to it by the apostles. Friday had been the day of man. On that day men had done everything which was done. It was by men that Jesus of Nazareth had been dragged before Pontius Pilate. By man he had been condemned. It was man who had thrust the crown of thorns down on his head. It was man who had buffeted him and scoffed at him. It was man who had nailed his hands to the cross, and it was man who had thrust the spear into his side. It was man who had laid him in the tomb, and had sealed the tomb, and had set a guard at the door of the tomb. Friday was the day of man. But on the first day of the week, God began to disclose his power. He revealed his plan, he made clear his purpose. He broke the bonds of death. He raised Jesus from the dead. He flooded the hearts of the disciples with light and joy. From that day to this, the first day of every week has been to every Christian heart the day of the Lord. Easter is the anniversary of that resurrection day. On Easter we bring out our brightest flowers and our sweetest songs. By these we symbolize our dearest hopes. The risen Christ dwells in our hearts, and he is the hope of glory.

This is the day of the Lord, and it points forward to another day, a brighter and a greater Day which is coming. Beyond death we shall enter upon a higher and more wonderful Day of the Lord. The sun of that day will never set. In that day we shall see more clearly than we see here God's purposes and plans. In that day we shall know more fully the extent of his power, the reach of his wisdom, and the depth of his love. That will be a day of blessedness supreme. Language cannot describe it. Imagination cannot picture it. Eye has not seen, ear has not heard, nor is it within the power of the mind of man to conceive the things which God has prepared for those who love him.

APPENDIX

QUESTIONS ON THE FIRST THIRTY-NINE CHAPTERS OF THE BOOK OF ISAIAH

For the Use of Bible Classes

1. What is the root meaning of the word "Prophet?"
2. Contrast the prophets of Isaiah's time with those of today.
3. How does Isaiah rank among the prophets of Israel?
4. When did he live? Three important dates in his life?
5. Draw a rough map of the world which he knew.
6. What prophets preceded him? Who was a contemporary prophet?
7. What did he add to the teachings of his predecessors?
8. Conspicuous traits of his character?
9. The strongest powers of his mind?
10. Characteristics of his style?
11. His message to his generation?
12. What great hymn based on a chapter in Isaiah?
13. Ten facts that we know of his life?
14. What does tradition report of his death?
15. Is his death referred to in any New Testament Book?
16. Is he quoted in any Old Testament Book?
17. How often does Jesus quote him? Peter? John? Paul?
18. Was he sensational in his methods?

19. What does Paul say of him?
20. Was he a visionary? How many of his visions are recorded?
21. The difference between a priest and a prophet? A prophet and a reformer? A prophet and a preacher?
22. What was the early notion of holiness? The later?
23. Where does Isaiah remind one of Peter? of Diogenes?
24. Where is the width of his mind most clearly shown?
25. Was he an Idealist? An Internationalist?
26. How many Isaiahs are there?
27. How much of our book was written by the son of Amoz?
28. Why is the book hard to read? Who, mentioned in the Bible, tried to read it and failed?
29. How did it come into its present shape?
30. Does this book contain an apocalypse?
31. How does prophecy differ from apocalypse?
32. How does the composite authorship of a book affect our doctrine of inspiration?
33. Does anonymity weaken authority?
34. Why were other prophecies bound up with his?
35. How do you know he did not write the Ode on Babylon—Chapters XIII-XIV, 23?
36. Can we depend on Old Testament titles to chapters? On Old Testament chronology?
37. What and where is the Taylor Prism?
38. What is the Eponym Canon?
39. Name the Kings of Israel in Isaiah's day.
40. Name the contemporary Kings of Judah, Assyria, Egypt.
41. What King of Babylon is mentioned?

42. Was Isaiah a Politician? A Statesman?
43. Was his advice to Ahaz good or bad?
44. Depict the character of Ahaz. Of Hezekiah.
45. Foreign nations mentioned by Isaiah?
46. What is his attitude to them?
47. World forces in the eighth century B.C.?
48. How far was Jerusalem from Egypt? From Samaria? From Assyria?
49. Who was a second Solomon?
50. What was Isaiah's main problem?
51. Who was Ariel? Shebna? Eliakim? Rabshakeh?
52. Will the brute creation share in the benefits of man's redemption?
53. What four nations cannot Isaiah forgive?
54. What was the first article of his creed?
55. What cured Hezekiah?
56. What defeated Sennacherib? Name a famous poem on his overthrow.
57. Why does Isaiah call Egypt Rahab?
58. His most vivid images?
59. His most startling picture?
60. His most brilliant passages?
61. His greatest chapter? The most beautiful?
62. His most often quoted sentences?
63. Compare Isaiah's Parable of the Vineyard with that of Jesus.
64. What was the sin of Moab?
65. Explain the retreat of the shadow — Chapter XXXVIII, 8.
66. Isaiah's favorite name for God? Other names?
67. What is the peril of formalism?
68. What is his idea of Religion? Patriotism? Commerce?

69. Attitude of Hosea, Zechariah and Isaiah to War?
70. How will war be abolished?
71. Where are the seven spirits of God defined?
72. State the doctrine of the Remnant.
73. What text has been most used in the coronation of kings?
74. Who has been considered Isaiah's best commentator?
75. Will Zion ever be the center of God's people?
76. How many portraits by Isaiah of the Messiah? Compare them.
77. Is Isaiah's Messiah supernatural? Is he God?
78. Who was the mother of Immanuel? Was his conception supernatural?
79. Was that phophecy fulfilled?
80. Was Matthew justified in applying it to Jesus?
81. Name six prophecies of Isaiah not fulfilled.
82. Was Paradise behind or in front of him?
83. Are faith and reason hostile to each other?
84. Where does his faith fly highest?
85. Did he see the distant future? Did he foresee the exile?
86. Do ideals ever die? Why?
87. Where does he predict the fall of Jerusalem?
88. In what chapter is he most despondent?
89. Where did he fall below himself?
90. How did his teaching hamper Jeremiah?
91. His idea of entangling alliances? Your idea?
92. The sins of his age? Of ours?
93. What are the besetting sins of rich men? Of politicians?
94. What are the besetting sins of women?
95. What is his Gospel to women?

APPENDIX

96. Has he a message for the individual?
97. Did he teach Immortality?
98. In what respects was his age like our own?
99. What has he to teach us?
100. His supreme service to the world?